DEBBIE MACOMBER'S
Christmas Cookbook

Photographs by Andy Ryan

HARLEQUIN®

Debbie Macomber's Christmas Cookbook

ISBN-13: 978-0373-89239-6

© 2011 by Debbie Macomber
Photography © 2011 by Andy Ryan

www.Harlequin.com

Printed in U.S.A.

Book Design: Susi Oberhelman
Front cover photography: Michael Alberstedt
Back cover and interior photography: Andy Ryan
Food Stylist: Catrine Kelty
Recipe Developer: Susan Lilly Ott

Contents

Christmas and Christmas Eve Dinner

Introduction

Oh, how I love Christmas. Give me an excuse to prepare a spread for my family or invite friends to the house, and I immediately head for the kitchen and reach for my cookbooks. (I've lost count of the number I've collected through the years. Cookbooks dating back to my years as a young wife and mother, even a recipe file from my teen years. I have notes from my grand-mother, as well as my mother's recipes.)

What the holidays are really about is being with others. They're about celebrating and sustaining our personal community of family and friends, giving and receiving affection, recip-rocating good times—and that so often takes the form of a shared meal.

Every year, for almost as long as I've been published, I've written a book that features some aspect of Christmas. It was my love of Christmas that brought those wacky and irrepress-ible angels, Shirley, Goodness and Mercy, to life. That goes for Mrs. Miracle, too, along with dozens of holiday-themed stories. My goal was—and is—to give you, my readers, something to take you away from the frantic activity of the Christmas season and yet ultimately reflect what it really means. To give you the gift of laughter and a few moments of respite and relaxation.

What I love most about the Christmas holidays is the traditions with family and friends. When Wayne and I were first married, we lived in western Washington State and our families lived on the other side of the Cascade Mountains. Traversing the mountain passes in the dead of winter wasn't always possible, so we had to start our own traditions.

I'll be passing on several of those Macomber family traditions in this cookbook. Take what you like and add your own unique twist. I offer them to you with a grateful heart for all you've done to support me through my publishing career.

I can say without hesitation that you're going to enjoy this cookbook. The recipes will leave you eager to get into the kitchen; the pictures are a feast for the eyes and will inspire you.

Please join me now and flip through the pages. As you read these recipes and Christmas craft suggestions, remember you'll be creating memories in your own kitchen, sharing a heritage of good eating with your family and friends.

Merry Christmas from my family to yours!

Debbie Macomber

Merry Morning Breakfast

For many years, our tradition was to open gifts on Christmas morning. Maybe that's a tradition in your family, too.

Because they just couldn't wait, one or both of our boys would rise before dawn and tiptoe into the living room to sort through the gifts. Then someone would put on Christmas music, which naturally woke us all up. Before long, the frenzy would begin.

First thing Christmas morning (like every morning!), my husband, Wayne, needed his coffee in order to function. While he waited for the coffee to brew, I put the breakfast casserole in the oven to bake. Then and only then was the opening of gifts permitted. (I assembled the casserole the night before and stuck it in the refrigerator. You'll find the recipe in this chapter.)
We never let our children just rip into their gifts. We did things in an orderly fashion, taking turns; everyone had an opportunity to choose which present he or she would open next.

I particularly remember the year Ted was five. He'd get so excited when it was his turn, he'd race around the package two or three times before he opened it. Come to think of it, he still does. (Just kidding!)

It always seemed that the casserole finished baking before we were through opening gifts, so we'd take a break and concentrate on breakfast. What I remember most about those Christmas breakfasts wasn't the meal itself (delicious though it was); what lingers in my mind is the conversation around the table. The laughter and stories and jokes. No one was in a rush. No one had an appointment that required a quick bite and then dashing out the door. No one had someplace else they needed to be. This was family time at its best.

My childhood memories of Christmas breakfast, any breakfast really, involve potato salad. You see, my father loved potato salad and we ate it at *every* holiday meal. In fact, I was a married adult before I learned that not all families had fried eggs and potato salad for breakfast. (Try it, though—it's really good.) For as long as I can remember, my mother made my father a huge batch of potato salad on Saturday that would have to last him the week. I don't think it ever went past Wednesday.

Over the years, Christmas morning has changed quite a bit for Wayne and me. These days, we're usually on the road, driving from Washington State to our winter home in Vero Beach, Florida. We've spent Christmas Day with friends Joan and Bob McKeon in Arizona and with Terry and Cheryl Adler, my brother and sister-in-law in Kansas City. But most often we're somewhere between Washington and Florida. It was hard for me to give up Christmas Day with our children and grandchildren. Now we celebrate with our family the weekend before—I'll tell you about that later. By leaving a few days ahead of the official holiday, Wayne and I have freed our children to establish new traditions with their own families.

The lesson I've learned from our experience is that traditions need to be flexible, need to change with the times, adapt to circumstances. In my book *Can This Be Christmas?* a group of travelers is stranded in a train depot on Christmas Eve. After getting over the initial shock of not being able to reach their families, not being able to take part in their usual traditions, they become family to one another for that one night.

Years ago, I never dreamed I'd be on the road on Christmas Day without my children or grandchildren. Wayne and I have had Christmas breakfasts in truck stops and small cafés all across the United States. What I find universal, however, is the camaraderie shared in these places, the goodwill and friendliness that permeates the day, no matter where we might be.

Candy Cane Sweet Bread Braid

SERVES 16

DOUGH

6 tablespoons (3 ounces) warm water

1 package (0.25 ounce) rapid-rise or instant yeast

1 teaspoon plus ⅓ cup granulated sugar

¼ cup plus 2½ cups all-purpose flour

6 tablespoons (3 ounces) sour cream or plain yogurt

4 tablespoons (½ stick) unsalted butter, at room temperature, plus more for bowl

1 large egg plus 1 egg, beaten with 1 teaspoon water, for egg wash

1 teaspoon salt

1 teaspoon vanilla extract

Large-grain sparkling white sugar

FILLING

3 ounces cream cheese, at room temperature

2 tablespoons granulated sugar

2 tablespoons sour cream or heavy cream

2 tablespoons all-purpose flour

1 teaspoon fresh lemon juice

¼ cup raspberry jam

Don't be discouraged by the number of steps in this recipe; it's actually very easy to put together. If you like, you can stop after step 5, cover the braid with plastic wrap and either refrigerate it overnight, or freeze it for up to a week. Bring back to room temperature before continuing with recipe.

1 For dough: In a small glass measuring cup, combine water, yeast, 1 teaspoon of the sugar and ¼ cup of the flour. Cover with plastic wrap and let sit for 10 minutes.

2 In a large bowl with electric mixer on medium speed, stir the yeast mixture, sour cream, butter, 1 egg, remaining ⅓ cup sugar, salt and vanilla. Add remaining 2½ cups flour; mix for 5 minutes, until a dough forms. Using lightly floured hands, scoop the dough up and form into a ball. Butter bottom and side of a large bowl. Place dough in bowl; turn dough to coat with butter. Cover bowl with plastic wrap; place in a warm spot and let rise for 1 hour, until nearly doubled.

3 For filling: In a small bowl, combine all filling ingredients, except jam, until smooth.

4 Line a baking sheet with parchment paper. Turn dough out onto a lightly floured surface; roll dough into a 10-by-15-inch rectangle. Transfer dough to prepared baking sheet. Using a sharp knife, create light indentations that divide the dough into three columns, lengthwise. Spread the cream cheese filling down the center section, leaving a 2-inch border on the top and bottom. Spread the jam over the cream cheese filling.

5 To form the braid, cut crosswise strips 1 inch apart down the length of the outer columns of the dough (the parts without filling). There should be an equal number of 1-inch strips on either side. Remove the four corner segments on the top and bottom. Fold the top middle (unfilled) flap down and the bottom middle flap up over the filling. Lift the top dough strip on the right side and bring it diagonally across the filling. Repeat on the left side, bringing the strip across the previous strip from the other

side. Continue down the entire braid, alternating strips. Gently stretch the whole weaved dough into a longer piece. Pull and turn the upper portion to form the hooked top of the candy cane. Cover bread loosely with plastic wrap; let rise in a warm place for 45 to 60 minutes, until puffy.

6. Preheat oven to 375°F. Brush bread with egg wash and sprinkle with sparkling sugar. Bake for 25 minutes, or until baked through and golden brown.

> **TIP:** If you bake often, buy a container of large-grain sparkling white sugar (sometimes called pearl sugar) to sprinkle on sweet breads or cookies. Although the grains are large, they soften upon baking.

Also shown on page 17.

Cinnamon-Sugar Monkey Bread

This old-fashioned, classic yeasted bread makes a spectacular addition to your holiday table. Cut into warm slices or let more adventurous diners pull off the sweet dough balls with their fingers.

1. Generously butter and lightly flour a large Bundt pan. Butter a large bowl that will hold the dough while it rises.

2. For dough: In a large glass measuring cup, combine warm milk, water, melted butter, granulated sugar and yeast. Let sit for 2 minutes. In a large bowl with electric mixer on low speed, stir flour and salt. With the mixer running, pour in milk mixture. Increase speed; beat for 3 minutes, until dough is smooth. The dough will be moist; if too sticky, add up to 2 tablespoons flour to make it kneadable.

3. On a lightly floured surface, knead dough to form a smooth ball. Place dough in buttered bowl; turn ball to coat with butter. Cover bowl with plastic wrap; place in a warm spot and let rise 1 hour, until nearly doubled.

4. For coating: In a small bowl, combine brown sugar and cinnamon. Place melted butter in a second bowl.

5. On a lightly floured surface, roll dough into a rough square about ½-inch thick. Using a sharp knife, cut dough into 64 pieces. Gently roll each piece into a ball; dip ball into melted butter, allowing excess butter to drip back into bowl. Roll balls in brown sugar mixture; place in prepared baking pan, piling balls in pan so that there are no gaps.

6. Cover pan tightly with plastic wrap; place in a warm spot and let rise for 1 hour, until dough rises to about 2 inches from the top of the pan.

7. Preheat oven to 350°F. Remove plastic; bake for 30 to 35 minutes, until top is deep brown and caramel begins to bubble around edges. Cool in pan for 5 minutes, then turn out on platter and cool for 10 minutes.

8. For glaze: In a small bowl, whisk confectioners' sugar and milk until smooth. Using whisk, drizzle glaze over top and sides of warm bread.

DOUGH

1 cup whole milk, warmed

⅓ cup warm water

2 tablespoons unsalted butter, melted, plus more for pan

⅓ cup granulated sugar

1 package (0.25 ounce) rapid-rise or instant yeast

3¼ cups all-purpose flour

1 teaspoon salt

COATING

¾ cup light brown sugar

2 teaspoons ground cinnamon

½ cup (1 stick) unsalted butter, melted

GLAZE

1 cup confectioners' sugar

2 tablespoons half-and-half or whole milk

TIP: After baking, don't let the bread cool in the pan for more than 5 minutes or it will stick to the pan. Run a spatula around the outside of the bread before inverting the pan.

Giant Crumb Apple Pie Coffee Cake

SERVES 8 TO 10

CRUMBS

½ cup (1 stick) unsalted butter, melted

⅓ cup brown sugar

⅓ cup granulated sugar

½ teaspoon ground cinnamon

Pinch salt

1¾ cups all-purpose flour

CAKE

⅓ cup light or regular sour cream or buttermilk

1 large egg plus 1 yolk

1 tablespoon vanilla extract

1 cup all-purpose flour

½ cup granulated sugar

½ teaspoon baking soda

½ teaspoon baking powder

¼ teaspoon salt

6 tablespoons (¾ stick) unsalted butter, at room temperature and cut into chunks, plus more for pan

FILLING

1 large Granny Smith or Green Delicious apple, peeled and very thinly sliced

2 tablespoons granulated sugar

½ teaspoon ground cinnamon

This big cake, loaded with buttery crumbs, is a can't-miss combination of apple pie and crumb cake.

1. Preheat oven to 325°F. Line an 8- or 9-inch springform pan with parchment paper. Butter paper and up the sides of the pan.

2. For crumbs: In a medium bowl, combine melted butter, *both* sugars, cinnamon and salt; stir until smooth. Stir in flour until batter forms into a thick mass.

3. For cake: In a small bowl, whisk sour cream, egg, yolk and vanilla until blended. In a large bowl with electric mixer, mix flour, sugar, baking soda, baking powder and salt. Add butter chunks; beat until blended. Gradually add sour cream mixture, stopping to scrape down the sides of bowl to evenly blend batter. Spread batter evenly into prepared pan.

4. For filling: In a medium bowl, toss apple slices with sugar and cinnamon. Layer apple slices in concentric circles over batter. Using your fingers, break crumb mixture into big chunks; sprinkle over apples. Bake for 50 minutes, until apples are cooked and a toothpick inserted into center comes out with moist crumbs. Transfer to a wire rack to cool completely.

TIP: Be sure to slice the apple very thinly so it cooks through in the baking time.

Chewy Fruit and Nut Granola Bars

MAKES ABOUT 12

1²⁄₃ cups quick-cooking oatmeal

2 tablespoons granulated sugar

¹⁄₃ cup oat flour (or ½ cup oats, processed till finely ground in a food processor or blender)

¼ teaspoon salt

¼ teaspoon ground cinnamon

1 cup toasted chopped nuts, your choice

1 cup raisins, dried cranberries and/or chopped dates

1 cup sweetened or unsweetened coconut flakes

5 tablespoons unsalted butter, plus more for pan

¼ cup honey or maple syrup

1 tablespoon corn syrup

1 tablespoon water

1 teaspoon vanilla extract

This is an incredibly flexible recipe—use any type of nut or dried fruit that your family likes. Although these bars are a nutritious addition to your holiday breakfast, they also make great lunchbox fillers or after-school snacks.

1. Preheat oven to 350°F. Line an 8- or 9-inch square baking pan with parchment paper or foil, pressing paper so that it fits into pan. Lightly butter paper.

2. In a large bowl, combine the first 8 ingredients. In a glass measuring cup or bowl, combine butter and honey; microwave until butter is melted and honey is warm. Stir corn syrup, water and vanilla into melted butter mixture. Toss warm liquid ingredients with oat mixture until evenly coated.

3. Spread batter into the prepared pan, pressing it firmly into the corners of the pan (batter will be sticky). Bake for 35 to 40 minutes, until golden around the edges, but still soft in the center. Transfer to a wire rack to cool. Let cool completely before lifting bars from pan.

TIP: It is very important to let the bars cool completely before you attempt to cut them. If cut warm, the bars will crumble. To assure a clean cut, refrigerate the bars until cold.

Mini Pain au Chocolat

Thanks to frozen puff pastry, these sweet treats, perfect for the littlest holiday guests, couldn't be easier to put together.

MAKES 14

1. Preheat oven to 375°F. Line a baking sheet with parchment paper.

2. On a lightly floured surface, roll out pastry into a 14-by-10-inch rectangle; cut in half lengthwise. Using a sharp knife, diagonally cut each rectangle into 7 triangles. Place about 10 chocolate chips on the wide end of each triangle. Starting from the base end, roll up the triangles toward the point. Place the pastries, point-side down on the prepared baking pan. Slightly curl the edges toward each other to form a crescent shape. Brush with egg wash. Bake for 15 minutes, until golden brown. Transfer to a wire rack to cool.

½ pound (1 sheet) frozen puff pastry, thawed according to package directions

⅔ cup (about) semisweet chocolate chips or chopped semisweet chocolate

1 egg yolk whisked with 1 tablespoon heavy cream, for wash

TIP: Croissants are best eaten the day they are made. They are best stored frozen in a resealable bag and reheated.

Tropical Paradise Muffins

MAKES 18

MUFFINS

3 cups all-purpose flour

1½ cups granulated sugar

2 teaspoons baking powder

1 teaspoon baking soda

½ teaspoon ground cinnamon

½ teaspoon salt

6 tablespoons (¾ stick) unsalted butter, melted

2 large eggs

¾ cup whole milk or buttermilk

2 teaspoons vanilla extract

1 cup mashed ripe bananas (about 3 bananas)

1 cup chopped macadamia nuts or skinned hazelnuts

1 cup sweetened coconut flakes

TOPPING

¼ cup sweetened coconut flakes

¼ cup chopped dried bananas

1 tablespoon granulated sugar

2 tablespoons chopped macadamia nuts or skinned hazelnuts

Like a trip to a tropical island in the middle of winter, these little cakes make for a sweet snack any time of the day.

1. Preheat oven to 350°F. Line 18 large muffin cups with paper liners.

2. For muffins: In a large bowl with electric mixer on low speed, stir the flour, sugar, baking powder, baking soda, cinnamon and salt. In a medium bowl, whisk melted butter, eggs, milk, vanilla and mashed bananas until combined. Stir banana mixture into dry ingredients until just blended; don't overmix. Fold in nuts and coconut. Spoon the batter into the paper liners, filling each cup about ¾ of the way.

3. For topping: In a small cup, combine coconut, dried bananas, sugar and chopped nuts; sprinkle over muffins. Bake for 23 to 25 minutes, or until golden and a toothpick inserted in center comes out clean. Transfer to a wire rack; let cool for 10 minutes. Carefully lift muffins from pan.

TIP: To quickly fill muffin cups with less mess, pour the batter from a measuring cup.

Orange Sweet Rolls with Cream Cheese Glaze

If you think you are not the type to make cinnamon rolls from scratch, think again. Although the recipe takes time, the steps are easy and the results delicious.

MAKES 12

1. For dough: In a large bowl with electric mixer on low speed, stir yeast and warm milk. Let sit for 2 minutes. Add butter, sugar, vanilla and 1 cup of the flour; stir until just combined. Add salt, cinnamon and orange zest. Add eggs and remaining flour; beat until a sticky dough forms.

2. Switch to the dough hook of mixer; beat for about 5 minutes, or until dough is smooth and elastic. (Alternatively, turn dough out onto a lightly floured countertop and knead for 5 minutes.)

3. Butter bottom and sides of a large bowl. Scrape dough into bowl; turn dough to coat with butter. Cover bowl with plastic wrap; place in a warm spot and let rise 1 hour, until nearly doubled.

4. For filling: In a medium bowl, combine brown sugar and cinnamon. Lightly butter a 13-by-9-inch baking dish. Turn dough out onto a lightly floured surface; roll into a 10-by-15-inch rectangle. Spread evenly with the softened butter; sprinkle with the brown sugar filling. Starting from the long end, tightly roll up the dough into a long log. Cut the log into 12 equal rolls; place rolls in the prepared baking dish. Cover the pan with plastic wrap; let rise for 1 hour or until nearly doubled.

5. Preheat oven to 350°F. Remove plastic wrap; bake for 35 minutes, until lightly brown and firm to the touch.

6. For glaze: In a small bowl (or with a mixer), beat cream cheese until light and fluffy. Whisk in juice and confectioners' sugar until smooth. Spread glaze over warm rolls.

TIP: To make ahead, complete recipe through step 4. Cover the pan tightly with plastic wrap and refrigerate overnight. Remove from the refrigerator 1 hour before finishing the recipe.

DOUGH

1 package (0.25 ounce) rapid-rise or instant yeast

¾ cup whole or lowfat milk, warmed

½ cup (1 stick) unsalted butter, at room temperature, plus more for the pan

¼ cup granulated sugar

2 teaspoons vanilla extract

4¼ cups all-purpose flour

½ teaspoon salt

½ teaspoon ground cinnamon

1 tablespoon grated orange zest

2 large eggs, at room temperature

FILLING

1 cup light brown sugar

1 tablespoon ground cinnamon

4 tablespoons (½ stick) unsalted butter, at room temperature

GLAZE

4 ounces cream cheese, at room temperature

2 tablespoons orange juice

1 cup confectioners' sugar

Banana Nutella Crêpe Cake

SERVES 6

CRÊPES

¾ cup all-purpose flour

½ cup granulated sugar

¼ teaspoon salt

2 large eggs and 1 egg yolk

1¼ cups whole milk

1 teaspoon vanilla extract

4 tablespoons (½ stick) melted butter, for the pan

FILLING

Chocolate-hazelnut spread, such as Nutella

Bananas, sliced

Confectioners' sugar

This multilayered breakfast treat only looks complicated. It's as easy to make as a stack of pancakes.

1. For crêpes: In a food processor, pulse flour, sugar and salt until combined. Add eggs and yolk; process until blended. With the motor running, slowly pour in milk and vanilla; process until smooth. Refrigerate batter for 15 minutes, or up to overnight.

2. Warm a 9-inch nonstick skillet over medium heat. Add just a bit of butter to coat the pan. Pour about 3 tablespoons of batter into hot pan; pick up pan and swirl it around to evenly spread batter. Place back on heat; cook for 30 seconds. Using a spatula and fingers, flip crêpe; cook for 30 seconds. Crêpe should be almost firm to the touch and spotty brown. Transfer to a cutting board. Repeat process with remaining batter to make about 10 crêpes. (You may have extra crêpes; add them to the stack.)

3. Preheat broiler. Line a baking sheet with parchment paper. Layer two crêpes on prepared pan. Spread a thin layer of Nutella onto the top crêpe; add a few banana slices. Top with another crêpe and layer more Nutella and bananas. Repeat this process with remaining crêpes. Top with a final crêpe. Place baking sheet under broiler until cake is warmed through. Sprinkle cake with confectioners' sugar.

TIP: Crêpe batter can be made up to 2 days in advance. Store tightly covered in the refrigerator.

Apple and Sharp Cheddar Scones

MAKES 6

2 cups all-purpose flour

3 tablespoons granulated sugar

2 teaspoons baking powder

¼ teaspoon salt

6 tablespoons (¾ stick) cold unsalted butter, cut into chunks

1 large egg, plus 1 beaten egg, for egg wash

¼ cup heavy cream

2 tart apples, peeled, very thinly sliced and coarsely chopped

½ cup shredded sharp cheddar cheese

Since the baking time for these savory scones is short, make sure the apples are chopped fine, so they are cooked tender.

1. Preheat oven to 350°F. Line a baking sheet with parchment paper.

2. In a food processor, pulse flour, sugar, baking powder and salt until blended. Add butter pieces; pulse until mixture resembles fine crumbs. In a glass measuring cup, whisk 1 egg and cream until well blended; add to batter and pulse until just blended. Pulse in apple pieces and cheese.

3. Turn dough out onto a lightly floured surface. Knead dough just enough to assure ingredients are blended. Using floured hands, shape dough into a 1-inch thick round. Using a sharp knife, cut round into 6 wedges. Transfer to prepared baking sheet. Whisk remaining egg in a small bowl; brush over scones.

4. Bake for 25 to 30 minutes, until golden and firm to the touch. Transfer to a wire rack to cool.

TIP: An egg wash is brushed on top of the scones before baking to make the finished crust golden and shiny.

Bacon and Eggs Breakfast Pizza

Breakfast stand-by ingredients bacon and eggs take on a whole new life when piled atop a pizza crust and covered with melted cheese.

SERVES 4

1. Remove dough from refrigerator 30 minutes before baking. Adjust oven rack to the lowest position and set a pizza stone on it. Preheat oven to 425°F. Lightly dust a large baking sheet with cornmeal. On a lightly floured countertop, pat the dough into a disc. Roll dough to a 14-inch circle; transfer to prepared baking sheet.

2. Cook bacon in a large heavy skillet over medium heat until crisp. Transfer to a paper towel-lined plate to drain; crumble. Pour off all but 1 tablespoon of bacon drippings from skillet. Cook onion in bacon drippings for 5 minutes, until softened, stirring often.

3. Meanwhile, in a medium bowl, whisk eggs, salt and pepper. Add eggs to hot skillet; cook until almost done, stirring constantly. Remove from heat.

4. Sprinkle pizza dough with chopped bacon and ½ of the cheddar and mozzarella. Top evenly with scrambled eggs, then remaining cheese. Bake for 10 minutes, rotating pan halfway through baking time. Pizza is done when crust is golden and cheese is melted. Sprinkle with parsley and chives. Cut into wedges and serve immediately.

1 pound prepared pizza dough

Cornmeal, for dusting pan

6 strips bacon

½ medium onion, thinly sliced

6 large eggs

Salt and black pepper

¾ cup shredded cheddar cheese

¾ cup shredded mozzarella cheese

2 tablespoons chopped fresh parsley

2 tablespoons chopped fresh chives

TIP: Kids don't like herbs? Omit them. Want to add veggies? Sauté some red peppers along with the onions. Need more color? Top pizza with chopped tomatoes.

Ham and Swiss Quiche

Quiche is the perfect dish for entertaining, as it can be served warm or at room temperature.

1. Warm oil in a large, heavy skillet over low heat. Add onions; cook for 20 minutes, until softened and caramelized, stirring often.

2. Lay the thawed pie shell into a 9-inch pie pan, pressing down to fit dough into pan. Crimp the edges; refrigerate for 15 minutes.

3. Preheat oven to 350°F. In a medium bowl, whisk the sour cream and cream until combined. Whisk in eggs, nutmeg, salt and pepper.

4. Spread cooked onions evenly over pie shell. Layer ham and cheese over onions. Pour in egg mixture. Bake for 35 minutes, until puffed and just set in the middle. Transfer to a wire rack to cool. Serve warm or at room temperature.

TIP: Feel free to use your favorite homemade savory pie dough recipe here. You can also use a light sour cream. Stay away from the nonfat varieties though, as the quiche won't set properly.

SERVES 6 TO 8

1 tablespoon olive oil

1 medium onion, thinly sliced

1 refrigerated or frozen pie shell, thawed

1 cup light or regular sour cream

½ cup heavy cream

3 large eggs

Pinch ground nutmeg

Salt and black pepper

4 ounces diced cooked ham (such as Virginia or Black Forest)

1 cup shredded Swiss cheese

Buttermilk Biscuits with Smoked Salmon and Herb Cream Cheese

SERVES 8

BISCUITS

1¾ cups all-purpose flour, plus more for dusting

1 teaspoon baking powder

½ teaspoon baking soda

½ teaspoon salt

½ cup (1 stick) cold unsalted butter, diced

¾ cup buttermilk

2 teaspoons chopped fresh dill

1 egg, beaten with 2 teaspoons water, for egg wash

TOPPINGS

4 ounces cream cheese, at room temperature

1 tablespoon chopped fresh dill

4 ounces thinly sliced smoked salmon

1 medium tomato, thinly sliced

Thin slices red onion

Smoked salmon is classic brunch fare. Make it super-special by pairing it with herb-spiked cream cheese and homemade biscuits.

1. Preheat oven to 425°F. Line a baking sheet with parchment paper.

2. For biscuits: In a food processor, pulse flour, baking powder, baking soda and salt. Add butter and pulse to form coarse crumbs. Add buttermilk and dill; process until just combined. Turn dough out onto a lightly floured surface; press into a disc. Using floured hands, pat dough into a ¾-inch thick circle. Using a floured 2½-inch biscuit cutter, cut out biscuits and transfer to prepared baking sheet, spacing 2 inches apart. Gather remaining pieces of dough; reroll and cut biscuits. Brush tops with egg wash. Bake for 12 minutes, until firm and light golden brown.

3. In a medium bowl, stir softened cream cheese and dill until combined. On a platter, lay out the herbed cheese, salmon, tomato and onion. Split the warm biscuits and let diners fill them with the toppings of their choice.

TIP: It's easiest to separate the thin salmon slices when they are cold. For best flavor, let the fish sit at room temperature for at least 20 minutes before serving.

Zucchini Ribbon Frittata with Cheese

SERVES 6

8 large eggs

1 tablespoon chopped fresh thyme

1 tablespoon chopped fresh parsley

Salt and black pepper

1 cup shredded Jarlsberg or Swiss cheese

2 tablespoons olive oil

1 small onion, coarsely chopped

1 medium zucchini, trimmed, cut in half lengthwise, and thinly sliced (about 1½ cups)

1 medium fresh tomato, chopped

Once you've learned the basic technique for making a frittata, you're all set—as the seasons change, you can use any vegetable you like.

1 In a medium bowl, whisk eggs, thyme, parsley, salt, pepper and ¼ cup of the shredded cheese.

2 Warm oil in a medium nonstick skillet over medium heat; add onion and zucchini, cook for 8 minutes, until softened, stirring often. Stir in tomato. Pour egg mixture into hot pan and stir to combine ingredients. Reduce heat to low, cover skillet and cook for 12 to 14 minutes, until eggs are barely set.

3 Preheat broiler. Sprinkle frittata with remaining ¾ cup cheese. Broil 1 minute, until lightly browned. Let cool slightly; run a rubber spatula around edges of the pan to loosen frittata. Tilt skillet and slide frittata onto a serving plate.

TIP: If you can't find a nice tomato at the market, use always-reliable cherry tomatoes.

Warm German Potato Salad

SERVES 8 TO 10

3 pounds yellow or red boiling potatoes, unpeeled, cut into wedges

Salt and black pepper

8 slices bacon

1 medium onion, chopped

3 tablespoons all-purpose flour

⅓ cup apple-cider vinegar

⅓ cup water

¼ cup granulated sugar

1 teaspoon Dijon mustard

2 celery stalks, thinly sliced

½ cup chopped fresh parsley

An Adler family tradition, this warm and hearty dish is a welcome addition to a winter brunch.

1. Bring a medium pot of water to boil. Add potato wedges and salt; cook for 12 to 14 minutes, until just cooked through but not mushy. Drain; place in large serving bowl.

2. Cook bacon in a large heavy skillet over medium heat until crisp. Transfer to a paper-towel–lined plate to drain; crumble. Pour off all but 2 tablespoons bacon drippings from skillet. Cook onions in bacon drippings for 5 minutes, until softened, stirring often. Add flour; cook for 2 minutes, stirring. Stir in vinegar, water, sugar, mustard, salt and pepper. Cook for 2 minutes, until blended and bubbling. Add sauce to potatoes; fold in celery, parsley and crumbled bacon. Mix carefully to prevent mashing the potatoes. Serve immediately.

TIP: The potatoes will best absorb the sweet and sour flavors of the sauce if tossed while still warm.

Overnight Sausage and Caramelized Onion Casserole

The beauty of this delicious meal is that it tastes best if allowed to sit overnight in the refrigerator before baking. This makes it perfect for holiday entertaining.

1. Lightly oil a 2-quart casserole. Add the cubed bread.

2. Warm oil in a large skillet over medium-low heat. Add onion, red pepper and salt. Cook for 8 minutes, until softened and lightly caramelized, stirring often. Add sausage; cook for 10 minutes, until evenly browned, stirring to break up clumps. Drain on a paper-towel–lined plate.

3. In a medium bowl, whisk eggs, milk, dry mustard, nutmeg, thyme and salt until combined.

4. Scatter sausage mixture over bread cubes. Sprinkle with ½ of the cheese, the egg mixture and the remaining cheese. Press down on the top gently, so that all of the bread cubes are soaked with the egg mixture. Cover and refrigerate overnight.

5. To bake: Preheat oven to 350°F. Bring the casserole to room temperature. Bake, uncovered, for 40 minutes, or until edges are bubbling, top is golden and casserole is warmed through.

TIP: If challah is unavailable, use a fluffy Italian loaf.

SERVES 8

1 tablespoon olive oil, plus more for pan

4 cups (loosely packed) day-old challah bread cubes (from about 5 thick slices)

1 medium onion, thinly sliced

1 small red pepper, diced

Salt

1 pound sweet pork sausage

6 large eggs

1 cup half-and-half or whole milk

½ teaspoon dry mustard

¼ teaspoon ground nutmeg

1 teaspoon fresh thyme leaves

2 cups shredded Swiss or Jarlsberg cheese

Deck the Halls

Sometimes the best decorating inspiration comes from nature. Bring winter's wonderland indoors to add holiday accents all through the house.

Create festive candleholders by lining simple tea saucers with bright red poinsettia leaves or rose petals. Place a long white taper in a small (preferably glass) candleholder and nestle into flowers, covering the holder with the petals and/or leaves.

Make a bobeche (a wax-catching collar) for your candle. To make: Using a green pipe cleaner, form a circle just larger than the diameter of your candle. Gather several small, short evergreen branches and a long piece of light, easily bendable floral wire. Begin by wrapping wire around a branch, then around pipe cleaner to affix branch to pipe cleaner. Without cutting wire, add another branch; wrap with wire to secure it to the pipe cleaner. Branches should overlap. Place candle in holder, slide evergreen collar down candle.

Buy extra bunches of herbs when shopping for your holiday meal. Use herb branches to decorate serving platters and appetizer dishes.

Make your own natural cornucopia by filling a wooden trug (or a long handle-less basket) with pine boughs, pinecones, hazelnuts, chestnuts and winter fruits such as pomegranates and kumquats. A tip: Soak pine boughs overnight in a bathtub or sink filled with warm water. Dry well before using. Needles will stay fresher for a longer time.

For an elegant look, line the bottom half of a glass vase with white river pebbles; add water and nestle white birch or white dogwood branches into the pebbles.

Housewarming Wreaths

The traditional pine wreath is beautiful but ubiquitous. Here, some unique wreaths you can make yourself.

For a jingly, lustrous doorknob decoration, create a small button-and-bell wreath. Using 16-gauge wire, form a circle about 5 inches in diameter. Make a small loop on one end of wire with needle-nose pliers. Starting at the other end, alternate threading small jingle bells and pearlized buttons onto the wire, tightly packing bells and buttons so wreath is fat. (We used about 50 bells and 20 buttons.) When the wire is full, join ends by forming a hook on the unlooped end, and hooking it through the loop. Pinch the hook closed with pliers. Add a bow or loop a ribbon to hang wreath.

Show off colorful Christmas cards by making a sweet card wreath. Using a glue gun, affix small wooden (or red and green) clothespins to a large (about 14-inch diameter) grapevine wreath (available online and at craft stores). Glue the pins about 1½ inches apart, alternating them so some cards will point inward and some outward. Clip cards with the pins. Loop a ribbon around wreath for hanging.

I consider Christmas the perfect opportunity to invite special friends to my house for holiday tea parties.

My Christmas Teas began about fifteen years ago with friends I made at our local swimming pool, where I do laps four mornings a week. I saw Rachel Williams in the grocery store one afternoon and was astonished to see that she wore glasses. It dawned on me then that none of us really knew what the others looked like in our everyday lives! So at the pool the next morning I invited everyone to my house for tea. It was a spur-of-the-moment idea that quickly spread to other areas of my life.

My swimming friends came over, and I served tea and cookies, and for the first few years that was all I did. It was simply fun to get together and chat. The men and women I swim with have become dear friends. And, yes, we look very different with our clothes on and our hair done.

Because the Swimmers' Tea was so successful, I turned to my knitting friends next. At the time there was no yarn store in Port Orchard and we had to travel to either Shelton or Silverdale for yarn. I decided it would be fun to invite the knitters I knew in my own area for a "show and tell" Knitters' Tea.

The first people I asked were the members of the knitting and crochet group at the Port Orchard Senior Center. Laura Early (who inspired the character of Charlotte in the Cedar Cove series) was, in effect, the group's leader, since she's an expert knitter and we all went to her for help and advice. I included other knitting friends and the owners of yarn stores in nearby towns. You can imagine what a gathering of "yarnaholics" is like!

My Christmas Teas started out with a few Christmas cookies and various kinds of tea, but later I added a more substantial menu plus . . . fruitcake.

Yup, fruitcake. I figure there are two kinds of people in the world. Those who love fruitcake and those who don't. I happen to fall into the first category. When I wrote *There's Something About Christmas*, which centered on the finalists in a fruitcake contest, I included three recipes. And while going through my own recipe collection and the one I inherited from my mother, I found a manila envelope filled with fruitcake recipes that Mom had clipped from magazines and newspapers.

At our house, Christmas just wouldn't be Christmas without homemade fruitcake. One year, my husband, Wayne, and I decided to bake Julia Child's recipe. He's not as committed a fruitcake fan as I am, but he thought it sounded intriguing and even went to the grocery and liquor stores with me to pick up the ingredients. And he had to admit he loved this special recipe.

In addition to having my friends over for holiday teas, I initiated a tradition with my grandchildren, starting with Jazmine, who's the oldest. Tea parties. I bring out Aunt Betty Stierwalt's hats from the 1940s through the 1990s, and each girl chooses a hat. (The boys, needless to say, have no interest in that part of the proceedings.) Naturally there's a plate of cookies and these are often cookies we've baked together. At Christmastime, the decorated sugar cookies work best; with them, I serve tea. Yes, real tea in real china cups (with lots of milk). And we chat. Our conversations almost always revolve around the questions the kids ask about my childhood and about their parents while they were growing up. There's plenty of laughter and giggling, and although the boys claim they only come for the cookies, they enjoy my stories as much as the girls do!

Cream Scones with Dried Figs and Cherries

MAKES 8

2 cups all-purpose flour

¼ cup granulated sugar, plus additional for sprinkling

1 tablespoon baking powder

½ teaspoon salt

12 tablespoons (1½ sticks) unsalted butter, cut into chunks

2 large eggs

½ cup heavy cream

¾ cup dried cherries or cranberries

½ cup dried figs, chopped

1 egg, beaten with 1 tablespoon cream, for wash

Making these in the food processor means the dough comes together in minutes. These are not very sweet—feel free to increase the sugar if desired.

1. Preheat oven to 375°F. Line a baking sheet with parchment paper.

2. In a food processor, pulse flour, sugar, baking powder and salt until combined. Add butter chunks; pulse until mixture resembles fine crumbs. In a glass measuring cup, whisk eggs and cream until well blended; add to batter and pulse until just combined. Pulse in dried cherries and figs.

3. Scrape dough out onto a lightly floured surface. Knead dough just enough to assure ingredients are combined. Using floured hands, shape dough into a ¾-inch-thick round. Using a sharp knife, cut round into 8 wedges. Transfer to prepared baking sheet. Brush scones with egg wash; sprinkle with sugar.

4. Bake for 20 to 25 minutes, until golden and firm to the touch. Transfer to a wire rack to cool.

> **TIP:** Like all quick breads, for a moist and tender crumb, take care to stir the batter until just blended.

Shown on page 47.

Green Goddess Chicken Tea Sandwiches

This vibrant green chicken salad makes an excellent brunch dish or an elegant tea sandwich. Punch up the color by adding some thin tomato slices.

1. For dressing: In blender or food processor, puree all dressing ingredients until smooth. Cover and refrigerate for up to 2 days.

2. For salad: Place chicken in a medium heavy saucepan; cover with water and set over medium-high heat. Bring to a simmer; cook for 10 minutes, or until chicken is just cooked. Transfer chicken to a medium bowl; let cool. Break or shred into 1-inch strips.

3. Add dressing to bowl; toss until chicken is coated. Season with salt, pepper or lemon juice as desired. Assemble sandwiches using chicken salad and arugula. Cut each sandwich into 4 triangles.

TIP: Don't fret about finely chopping the herbs and garlic; the food processor does all the hard work for you.

MAKES 4 SANDWICHES

DRESSING

¼ cup buttermilk

¼ cup mayonnaise

¼ cup sour cream

½ cup chopped fresh parsley

2 tablespoons snipped fresh chives

1 tablespoon fresh lemon juice

SALAD

3 boneless, skinless chicken breast halves, trimmed

Salt and black pepper

Fresh lemon juice

Baby arugula leaves

Very thin whole-wheat bread slices

Winter Tomato Pie

SERVES 4

½ cup mayonnaise

2 tablespoons fresh lemon juice

1 can (28 ounces) plum tomatoes

2 tablespoons chopped fresh basil or prepared basil pesto

2 tablespoons snipped fresh chives

¾ cup shredded sharp cheddar cheese

¾ cup shredded Monterey Jack cheese

1 refrigerated pie crust, thawed

1 large egg, beaten with 2 teaspoons water, for wash

Using shredded cheese, canned tomatoes and a prepared pie crust means this hearty savory pie is in the oven in 5 minutes. Serve it with a green salad for a great light supper.

1. Preheat oven to 400°F. In a small bowl, mix mayonnaise with lemon juice.

2. Drain tomatoes; transfer to a cutting board and cut into thick slices. Cover the bottom of a glass or ceramic pie tin with about half of the slices. Sprinkle with half of the herbs, half of the shredded cheese and half of the mayonnaise mixture. Add remaining tomato slices, and top with the rest of the herbs, cheese and mayonnaise mixture.

3. Unroll pie crust. (If crust is not big enough to cover the pie tin, roll it out to a 10-inch circle.) Set dough over filling; crimp edges with fingers to form decorative edges. Brush crust with egg wash. Bake for 35 minutes, or until crust is golden and filling is just bubbling. Serve warm.

TIP: Refrigerated pie crusts are super-easy and much less likely to be broken than the frozen varieties. Find them in the refrigerated section of most supermarkets.

Sweet Pepper and Spinach Quiche

SERVES 6

1 refrigerated pie crust, thawed

1 tablespoon olive oil

1 red bell pepper, diced

2 ounces baby spinach leaves
(1 big handful)

1 tablespoon minced shallot or
white onion

4 large eggs

¾ cup half-and-half

Salt and black pepper

1 cup shredded Gruyère or
Jarlsberg cheese

¼ cup crumbled feta cheese

The Christmas hues of red and green make this a colorful addition to your holiday tea party.

1. Preheat oven to 375°F. Unroll pie crust according to package directions; press into a pie pan. Crimp edges to form a decorative crust.

2. Warm oil in a heavy medium skillet over medium-low heat. Add diced pepper; cook for 8 minutes, until softened, stirring. Mix in spinach and shallot; cook for 2 minutes, until spinach wilts, stirring.

3. In a medium bowl, whisk eggs, half-and-half, salt and pepper until blended. Fold in pepper mixture. Sprinkle both cheeses into pie crust; pour egg mixture over cheese.

4. Place quiche on a baking sheet and bake for 40 minutes, until edges are golden but center still feels soft. Transfer to a wire rack to cool. Serve warm or at room temperature.

TIP: Any shredded or crumbled cheese will work in this recipe; feel free to use up any leftover cheeses lurking in your refrigerator.

Deep Dark Date Fruitcake

Dense and dark, redolent with citrus and nuts, this is a serious fruitcake. Traditionalists can substitute 1 cup chopped candied citrus peel for an equal amount of dates.

1. Preheat oven to 350°F. Butter and flour the bottom of a 9-by-5-inch loaf pan. In a small bowl, combine dates and ⅓ cup of the orange juice; let sit for at least 10 minutes. In a large bowl, combine flour, baking powder, baking soda, cinnamon, nutmeg, cloves and salt.

2. In a large bowl with electric mixer on medium speed, beat butter and sugar until blended. Scrape down the sides of the bowl. Reduce mixer speed to low; beat in egg, vanilla and orange zest. With mixer still on low, add flour mixture alternately with remaining ¾ cup of orange juice, beating only until just combined. Fold in pecans and dates with their liquid.

3. Pour batter into the prepared pan. Bake for 45 to 50 minutes, until a toothpick comes out clean. Cool in pan for 10 minutes; turn out onto a wire rack to cool completely.

TIP: Be sure to add the juice used to marinate the dates—it's full of flavor.

SERVES 10 TO 12

2 cups coarsely chopped dates (about 10 ounces pitted)

⅓ cup plus ¾ cup orange juice

2 cups all-purpose flour

2 teaspoons baking powder

½ teaspoon baking soda

1 teaspoon ground cinnamon

1 teaspoon ground nutmeg

¼ teaspoon ground cloves

1 teaspoon salt

4 tablespoons (½ stick) unsalted butter, at room temperature, plus more for pan

1 cup light brown sugar

1 large egg

1 teaspoon vanilla extract

1 tablespoon grated orange zest (from 2 oranges)

1 cup chopped toasted pecans

Bakery Window Lemon Poppy Seed Cake

SERVES 10

CAKE

½ cup sour cream

¼ cup poppy seeds

1 tablespoon grated lemon zest

1 tablespoon fresh lemon juice

¼ teaspoon lemon extract

1⅓ cups plus 1 tablespoon
all-purpose flour

¼ teaspoon baking soda

½ cup (1 stick) unsalted butter,
at room temperature, plus more
for pan

1½ cups granulated sugar

3 large eggs, at room
temperature

2 teaspoons vanilla extract

GLAZE

¼ cup fresh lemon juice
(from about 2 lemons)

¼ cup granulated sugar

Happily, this lemon-scented tea loaf tastes just as delicious the next day as it does warm from the oven.

1. For cake: Preheat oven to 350°F. Butter and flour a 9-by-5-inch loaf pan. In a small bowl, stir sour cream, poppy seeds, lemon zest, juice and extract.

2. In a medium bowl, combine flour and baking soda. In large bowl with electric mixer on high speed, beat butter and sugar until light and blended. Add the eggs, 1 at a time, beating well after each addition. Beat in vanilla. Alternately add flour mixture and sour cream mixture, beating until just blended. Do not overmix.

3. Pour batter into prepared pan. Bake for 55 minutes, until a toothpick inserted in center of cake comes out clean. Transfer to a wire rack; cool for 10 minutes.

4. For glaze: In a small saucepan over low heat, warm juice and sugar until sugar dissolves into a syrup. Invert cake onto wire rack. Using a toothpick, poke holes all over the cake; brush with some of the syrup. Set cake right side up, poke holes in top of cake and brush with remaining syrup. Cool completely on wire rack.

TIP: Remember to zest the lemons before juicing them.

Five-Minute Cranberry Walnut Cobbler

This homey dessert is so easy to make and so sweetly satisfying that you will make it again and again. Serve warm with whipped cream if you are feeling decadent.

1. Preheat oven to 350°F. In a 9-inch pie pan, combine cranberries, walnuts and ½ cup of the sugar; toss until coated.

2. In a medium bowl, whisk eggs, melted butter, remaining sugar and almond extract until blended. Fold in flour and salt until combined. Pour the batter over the cranberry mixture. Bake for 40 minutes, until crust is golden and fruit bubbles. Transfer to a wire rack to cool.

TIP: No cranberries? No problem. Substitute blueberries or strawberries, but cut the sugar added to the fruit in half.

SERVES 8

2½ cups fresh or frozen cranberries

¾ cup chopped walnuts

½ cup plus ¾ cup granulated sugar

2 large eggs

12 tablespoons (1½ sticks) unsalted butter, melted

¼ teaspoon almond extract

1 cup all-purpose flour

Pinch salt

Salted Almond Carmelita Bars

MAKES 30 BARS

3 cups plus 3 tablespoons all-purpose flour

3 cups instant oatmeal

1½ teaspoons baking soda

¼ teaspoon salt

1 pound (4 sticks) unsalted butter, at room temperature, plus more for pan

2 cups light brown sugar

1½ cups (1 16-ounce jar) caramel sauce or dulce de leche

1½ cups semisweet chocolate chips

1½ cups chopped salted roasted almonds, or any nut

Cut these super-rich treats into small squares for serving. Use any nut your family likes.

1. Preheat oven to 350°F. Line a 9-by-13-inch baking pan with a large sheet of foil. Lightly butter foil.

2. In a large bowl with electric mixer on low speed, stir 3 cups of the flour, oatmeal, baking soda and salt. Add butter and brown sugar; beat until blended.

3. Spread half of the dough evenly into prepared baking pan; pat until evenly spread in pan. Bake for 15 minutes.

4. In a small bowl, stir the caramel sauce with remaining 3 tablespoons of flour until blended. Evenly scatter half of the chocolate chips and nuts over par-baked crust. Dollop half of the caramel sauce on top. Scatter the remaining dough evenly into pan. Top with remaining caramel, chocolate chips and nuts. Bake for 35 to 40 minutes, or until the edges are set. Do not overbake; bars will still be soft in the middle. Transfer to a wire rack to cool.

TIP: Once cooled, bars can be kept in an airtight container at room temperature for up to 3 days or frozen for up to 1 month.

Glazed Lemon Thins

For a dazzling finish, top these crisp lemon cookies with sparkling large-grain sugar. Let the glaze dry completely before stacking or storing the cookies.

1. For cookies: In a small bowl, whisk lemon juice, egg yolk and vanilla until combined.

2. In a food processor, mix granulated sugar and zest until combined, about 30 seconds. Add flour, baking powder and salt; pulse until combined. Add butter pieces; process until mixture resembles fine cornmeal. With machine running, slowly pour juice mixture through feed tube. Process until dough forms a ball.

3. Transfer dough to a lightly floured counter; roll into a 2-inch-wide, 10-inch-long log. Wrap tightly in plastic. Refrigerate for at least 2 hours, until firm.

4. Preheat oven to 325°F. Line 2 baking sheets with parchment paper. Unwrap dough; slice into disks between ¼- and ½-inch thick. Place on prepared baking sheets, about 1 inch apart. Bake for 15 minutes, until edges just start to brown. Rotate sheet halfway through baking. Cool on baking sheet for 3 minutes; transfer to a wire rack to cool completely.

5. For glaze: In a medium bowl, whisk cream cheese and lemon juice until smooth. Gradually fold in confectioners' sugar until glaze reaches desired consistency. Frost cookies; sprinkle with large-grain sugar.

TIP: The cookie dough log can be refrigerated or frozen and then sliced and baked another day. Just wrap it tightly and refrigerate for up to 2 days or freeze for up to 2 months.

MAKES ABOUT 30

COOKIES

2 tablespoons fresh lemon juice

1 large egg yolk

½ teaspoon vanilla extract

¾ cup granulated sugar

2 tablespoons grated lemon zest

1¾ cups all-purpose flour

¼ teaspoon baking powder

¼ teaspoon salt

12 tablespoons (1½ sticks) cold unsalted butter, chopped

GLAZE

1 tablespoon cream cheese, at room temperature

2 tablespoons fresh lemon juice

1¼ cups confectioners' sugar

Large-grain white sugar crystals

Coconut Snowballs

MAKES 38

4¼ cups (about 12 ounces) sweetened coconut flakes

1 cup granulated sugar

½ teaspoon salt

¼ teaspoon baking powder

½ cup (1 stick) cold unsalted butter, chopped, plus more for pan

1 large egg

1 teaspoon vanilla extract

½ teaspoon coconut extract

1½ cups all-purpose flour

These are a must for any coconut lover on your gift list.

1 Preheat oven to 350°F. Line 2 baking sheets with parchment paper; lightly butter paper.

2 Place 1 cup of coconut on a shallow plate. In a food processor, pulse remaining 3¼ cups coconut, sugar, salt and baking powder until fine crumbs form. Add butter chunks; process until just combined. Add egg and *both* extracts; process just until blended. Add flour; pulse just until a dough forms. Do not overmix. Stop and scrape sides of bowl as needed.

3 Scoop and drop tablespoons of dough into coconut on plate. Roll dough to form round balls and cover with flakes. Place on prepared baking sheet, about 2 inches apart. Bake for 13 minutes, until coconut shreds are lightly golden. Cool on baking sheet for 2 minutes; transfer to a wire rack to cool completely.

TIP: The parchment paper must be greased or the cookies will stick. A no-fuss method: use the butter clinging to the butter wrapper.

Cinnamon Star Sugar Cookies

Of course you can make these in any shape you like, any time of the year. The kids can be in charge of sprinkling the cinnamon-sugar over the cookies. Not only are these delicious, but they can also be used to make tree ornaments.

1. For cookies: In a large bowl with electric mixer on high speed, cream butter and sugar until light and fluffy. Add egg and vanilla; beat until combined.

2. In a separate bowl, combine flour, baking powder, salt and cinnamon. Reduce mixer speed to low; beat in flour mixture until just combined. Shape dough into a disk; wrap and refrigerate for at least 2 hours or up to overnight.

3. Preheat oven to 325°F. Line 2 baking sheets with parchment paper. Remove dough from the refrigerator. Cut disk in half; cover remaining half. With floured rolling pin on a lightly floured surface, roll dough ¼-inch thick. Using star-shaped cookie cutters, cut dough into as many cookies as possible; reserve trimmings for rerolling. Place cookies onto prepared baking sheets, about 1 inch apart. (If making ornaments, use a wooden skewer to poke a hole in each cookie for hanging.) Repeat with remaining dough and rerolled scraps.

4. For topping: In a small bowl, combine sugar and cinnamon. Lightly brush egg white over cookies; sprinkle with cinnamon-sugar. Bake for 10 to 12 minutes (depending on size of cookies), until golden around the edges. Cool on baking sheet for 1 minute; transfer to a wire rack to cool completely.

TIP: Like most sugar cookies, these keep well. Store in an airtight container for up to 2 weeks.

MAKES 24

COOKIES

½ cup (1 stick) unsalted butter, at room temperature

1 cup granulated sugar

1 large egg

1 teaspoon vanilla extract

2 cups all-purpose flour

½ teaspoon baking powder

¼ teaspoon salt

½ teaspoon ground cinnamon

TOPPING

¼ cup granulated sugar

½ teaspoon ground cinnamon

1 egg white

Ten Ideas for Ten-Minute Décor

Holiday decorating doesn't have to be expensive or time consuming. Here, some quick and easy ways to make your home festive when budgets are small and time is short.

1. Fill a large glass or pottery bowl with red and green apples or pears.

2. Dangle translucent glass and crystal Christmas ornaments from a dining room chandelier. The ornaments will reflect the light and dazzle your diners.

3. Fill several small glass or crystal bowls with vintage Christmas candies. Look for ribbon candy (available online at www.hammondscandies.com, if not in local stores).

4. Drape twinkle lights from ceiling beams, along bookshelves or the tops of kitchen cabinets. Keep them on all day.

5. Bring a Christmas tree into the kitchen. Decorate a fragrant tree-shaped rosemary plant with holiday ribbons and tiny ornaments. Look for food-themed ornaments.

6. Invest in a set of Christmas-y kitchen dishtowels, pot scrubbers and sponges.

7. Fill a big glass salad bowl or silver serving bowl with Christmas bulbs. For a sophisticated look, stick to two coordinating solid colors, like blue and silver.

8. Start forcing paperwhite bulbs in mid-November for a Christmas bloom. These "just add water" white-flowering bulbs look especially elegant planted in white stones or clear glass marbles.

9. Pour whole cranberries into the bottom of a large glass flower vase. Fill with water and a Christmas bouquet or selection of evergreen branches.

10. Fill a rarely used fireplace with a collection of large white pillar candles. Vary the sizes and arrange candles in staggered rows.

Since our homes look so beautiful for Christmas, it makes sense to invite our family and friends to share in the celebrations—which usually involves feeding them! Appetizers are the perfect solution.

My appreciation for appetizers started with the Christmas Teas I organize for my swimming and knitting friends, which I've already told you about. As I mentioned, at first I served just tea and cookies. But I soon realized that many of my friends could attend this party only during their lunch breaks from work. That was when I created a more substantial menu, mostly of finger foods and easy-to-eat appetizers. (Wayne doesn't attend my teas but he makes sure I put some of the goodies aside for him to enjoy later.)

Appetizers fit the bill for other social events, too. For a number of years, my daughters and I held an annual Christmas Open House. It all began with our Christmas slumber parties (which didn't have much to do with slumber!). We each chose special cookie and candy recipes and stayed up late to bake, cook and chat. The girls tended to last longer than I did; I usually crashed around two in the morning, especially if someone brought out a bottle of wine. (That someone was generally Wayne.) Jody and Jenny Adele seemed to have energy to spare and often worked until well into the night. More recently, our Christmas slumber party has evolved into another, newer tradition that includes the grandchildren, which I'll describe in the chapter Cooking with Grandma.

The first time Jody, Jenny Adele and I baked all these wonderful treats, the question was how to use them. That spurred the idea of a Christmas Open House. The girls and I host it and we each invite the people we consider our dearest friends, coworkers and neighbors.

Naturally the grandchildren get involved in these events, answering the door and collecting coats and scarves. They pass around serving plates and make sure everyone has enough to eat and drink.

My sons, Ted and Dale, contribute to the festivities by serving as parking valets.

It's become a regular joke that when someone reaches for a cookie, I suggest they ask what time of night that particular cookie was baked. If it ended up in the oven after midnight, I might recommend our guest try something else! Fortunately, we always have a number of tasty appetizers available—including some of the ones in this chapter.

Unlike many writers, I work out of an office . . . and, get this: My office is above a yarn store *and* an ice cream parlor. As I often say, this is pretty darn close to Nirvana.

If you came to my office, you'd meet Renate Roth, my personal assistant, who's been with me for almost eighteen years. And you'd meet Heidi Pollard, Wanda Roberts, Carol Bass and my daughter Jenny Adele. If you've ever asked me a question through my website, you've likely gotten a reply from Heidi, who's worked with me for the past six years. Wanda's my bookkeeper, and Carol responds to reader questions that come by regular mail. Jenny Adele is my brand manager. Each of them is an important member of my staff. Because we have working relationships with other businesses in the area (*besides* the yarn store and ice cream parlor!), we hold a Christmas Open House at the office. It's a great excuse to spiff everything up. The stairway that leads up to the turret office where I work is lined with author portraits and signatures, which my guests find of interest. These portraits include Mark Twain, Charles Dickens, Ernest Hemingway, Harper Lee and Helen Keller. They're my heroes, and I think of them as mentors. I see their smiling faces as I climb the stairs and feel that they're watching over me as I write.

At the office Open House—just like the one at my home—we serve some delicious appetizers. In *Call Me Mrs. Miracle*, Lindy Lee orders Holly to throw a Christmas party for her staff at the very last minute. Emily Merkle (aka Mrs. Miracle) saves the day by suggesting Holly contact the women at Heavenly Delights, who provide a selection of finger foods, appetizers and desserts that—true to their name—delight everyone.

I encourage you to share *these* heavenly appetizers with the special friends in your life—at Christmas and at every other occasion!

Deviled Crab Cakes with Chive Cream

MAKES 24

¼ cup mayonnaise

3 tablespoons snipped fresh chives

1 tablespoon fresh lemon juice

1 teaspoon honey

1 teaspoon Worcestershire sauce

½ teaspoon dry mustard

12 ounces crab meat (fresh or canned and drained)

Salt and cayenne pepper

¾ cup Panko or other fine bread crumbs

TOPPINGS

Sour cream

Paprika

Snipped fresh chives

These are bite-sized cakes. For heartier appetizers, form bigger cakes and bake them longer.

1. In a large bowl, combine first 6 ingredients. Fold in crab meat, salt and cayenne pepper. Stir in 4 tablespoons of bread crumbs until mixture just holds together. Place remaining bread crumbs in a shallow bowl.

2. Roll crab mixture into large walnut-sized balls. Drop balls into bread crumbs in bowl; gently roll balls until coated. Place on a baking sheet; gently press to flatten slightly. Cover with plastic wrap and refrigerate for at least 30 minutes or up to 24 hours.

3. Preheat oven to 400°F. Remove plastic; bake for 20 minutes, until crisp, golden and warmed through.

4. Top cakes with a tiny dollop of sour cream, a sprinkle of paprika and minced chives.

TIP: Remember to pick over the canned crab meat to make sure there are no tiny pieces of shell.

Shown on page 67.

Roast Beef and Baby Arugula Toasts

These elegant bites are really just a few great ingredients piled on top of crispy toasts. The red pepper mixture can be made 1 day ahead and stored in the refrigerator. The toasts can be baked a few days in advance.

1. Preheat oven to 300°F. Place baguette slices on a baking sheet; brush with oil. Bake for 15 minutes, until lightly golden and crisp. Let cool; spread with half of the goat cheese.

2. In a small bowl, combine red peppers, thyme and vinegar. Top toasts with folded roast beef, a small mound of the red pepper mixture and an arugula leaf. Dot with reserved goat cheese. Season to taste with salt and pepper.

TIP: Tiny curls of baby arugula are the perfect topping for these appetizers. Other options: a sprig of frisée lettuce or a parsley leaf.

MAKES 16

16 thin diagonally cut baguette slices

Olive oil

4 tablespoons crumbled goat cheese

¼ cup thinly sliced roasted red peppers (from a jar)

1 teaspoon chopped fresh thyme

½ teaspoon sherry or red-wine vinegar

16 very thin slices rare roast beef

16 baby arugula leaves

Salt and black pepper

Caesar Salad Bites

MAKES ABOUT 24

1 cup finely diced white bread (from about 2 slices)

1 tablespoon olive oil

Salt and black pepper

¼ cup prepared Caesar salad dressing

1 tablespoon fresh lemon juice

3 tablespoons grated Parmesan cheese

2 heads Belgian endive

Garnishes: croutons, grated cheese

America's favorite party salad goes portable, thanks to crunchy endive boats.

1. Preheat oven to 350°F. In a medium bowl, toss bread cubes with oil; season with salt and pepper. Spread cubes on a rimmed baking sheet. Bake 6 to 8 minutes, until toasted and crisp, stirring occasionally.

2. Meanwhile, in same bowl (no need to wash), stir salad dressing, lemon juice and 1 tablespoon of Parmesan until blended.

3. Trim tough ends from endive; peel off about 24 of the largest leaves from heads. Stack leaves; trim stack so each leaf is about 4 inches long. Chop remaining endive heads, along with trimmings from stacks. Add chopped endive to the bowl with remaining 2 tablespoons of Parmesan; toss to coat. Spoon salad onto each endive spear. Garnish with croutons and grated cheese.

TIP: Cut the bread for croutons into very small cubes; premade croutons are just too big for these little bites.

Spanish Tortilla with Crispy Bacon

Serve this always-satisfying dish just about any time—as an appetizer at a cocktail party, an entrée for a light supper or a hearty brunch main dish.

① In a 10-inch nonstick skillet over medium heat, cook bacon until crisp. Transfer to a paper-towel–lined plate to drain. Coarsely chop.

② In a large bowl, toss 1 tablespoon of the oil, sliced potatoes, onion, and salt and pepper until potatoes are coated. Warm bacon drippings in same skillet over medium-high heat until shimmering. Reduce heat to medium-low and add potato mixture. Cover and cook for 25 minutes, until potatoes are tender, stirring every 5 minutes.

③ In same large bowl (no need to wash), whisk eggs, salt and thyme until blended. Stir in bacon. Add egg mixture to potatoes in skillet and cook for 30 seconds, shaking pan and gently stirring mixture. Reduce heat to medium, cover and cook for 6 minutes, gently shaking pan every 30 seconds. The top should be just set and no longer wet to the touch.

④ Run a rubber spatula around edges of skillet to loosen tortilla. Shake pan back and forth; the tortilla should slide around in pan. Place tortilla onto a large plate. Put another large plate over tortilla; invert plates so that the browned side is up. Slide tortilla, browned-side up, back into skillet. Set skillet over medium heat. Cook for 5 minutes, until bottom is golden and eggs are cooked through, gently shaking pan often. Slide tortilla onto cutting board. Cut into squares or wedges.

SERVES 8

4 slices bacon

1 tablespoon plus 1 teaspoon olive oil

1 pound (about 4 medium size) boiling potatoes (such as Yukon Gold), halved lengthwise and thinly sliced

1 small onion, very thinly sliced

Salt and black pepper

8 large eggs

1 teaspoon chopped fresh thyme

TIP: The skin on a Yukon Gold potato is so thin that there is no need to peel it.

Warm Spinach and Artichoke Dip with Garlic Crostini

Now that tender baby spinach is so readily available, there's no need to hassle with thawing and draining frozen spinach in order to make this much-loved dip.

1. For dip: Preheat oven to 375°F; position rack in center of oven. In food processor, combine artichoke hearts, shallot, garlic, cream cheese, sour cream, mayonnaise, Parmesan cheese and salt and pepper. Pulse until just combined, scraping down the sides of the bowl. Gradually add spinach to bowl, one big handful at a time, until all the leaves are blended.

2. Scoop mixture into a 2-quart casserole; sprinkle with mozzarella cheese. Bake for 25 minutes, until the cheese is melted and dip is warmed through. Serve warm.

3. For crostini: Pour oil into a small cup; add smashed garlic clove and let sit for 5 minutes. Preheat oven to 300°F. Place bread slices on a baking sheet; brush with garlic oil. Bake for 10 to 15 minutes, until lightly golden and crisp.

TIP: Add the spinach a handful at a time; the whole bag won't fit in the bowl of the food processor all at once.

SERVES 16

DIP

1 can (14 ounces) artichoke hearts, drained

½ small shallot, chopped

1 garlic clove, chopped

1 box (8 ounces) cream cheese, at room temperature

½ cup sour cream

⅓ cup mayonnaise

½ cup grated Parmesan cheese

Salt and black pepper

1 bag (8 ounces) baby spinach leaves

½ cup shredded mozzarella or Monterey Jack cheese

CROSTINI

¼ cup olive oil

1 garlic clove, smashed

20 thin, diagonally cut baguette slices

Prosciutto and Sun-Dried Tomato Pinwheels

MAKES ABOUT 55

1 sheet frozen puff pastry, thawed according to package directions

⅓ cup sun-dried tomatoes (packed in oil), drained and finely diced

2 ounces thinly sliced prosciutto, cut into thin strips

¼ cup shredded fontina or Swiss cheese

2 tablespoons grated Parmesan cheese

Black pepper

1 egg beaten with 1 teaspoon of water, for egg wash

Use this recipe as a starting point—feel free to alter the filling as you like. Some ideas: roasted red peppers and salami, ham and whole-grain mustard.

1. On a lightly floured surface, roll out thawed pastry to a 10-by-15-inch rectangle; cut in half lengthwise. Spread a thin layer of the tomatoes on both rectangles, leaving a ½-inch border around the edges. Top with prosciutto strips, fontina and Parmesan cheese. Season with pepper.

2. Starting at the near long edge, tightly roll the pastry pieces into two long logs. Brush long borders with egg wash; press to seal closed. Transfer logs to a large baking sheet and freeze for 30 minutes until firm.

3. Line 2 large baking sheets with parchment paper. Trim the uneven ends from each log. Cut on the diagonal into ¼-inch-thick slices; set pinwheels 1 inch apart on baking sheets. Freeze until firm.

4. Preheat oven to 375°F. Bake for 20 minutes, until lightly golden. Serve warm.

TIP: The frozen sliced pinwheels can be stored in a resealable plastic bag and frozen for up to 1 month.

Green Pea Hummus with Everything Pita Crisps

Inspire your guests with a party dip that's actually nutritious. For best flavor, use extra-virgin olive oil.

1. For hummus: In food processor, pulse all ingredients until smooth. Transfer to a serving bowl.

2. For pita crisps: Preheat oven to 350°F. Arrange pita wedges on a baking sheet, cut-side up. Lightly coat with oil spray. Sprinkle with poppy and sesame seeds and salt. Bake for 16 minutes, until golden and crisp, turning sheet to bake evenly.

TIP: Hummus may be made up to 4 days in advance and stored in the refrigerator. Bring to cool room temperature and stir in warm water to loosen the texture if needed.

MAKES 36 CRISPS AND 1¾ CUPS DIP

HUMMUS

1 package (10 ounces) frozen baby sweet peas, thawed

½ cup canned drained chickpeas

½ cup grated Parmesan or Romano cheese

¼ cup extra-virgin olive oil

3 tablespoons fresh lemon juice

½ garlic clove, minced

Salt

CRISPS

3 pita rounds, each cut into 6 wedges, then split open (to make 36)

Olive oil cooking spray

1 tablespoon poppy seeds

2 teaspoons sesame seeds

2 teaspoons large-grain sea salt

Black Bean Tortilla Cups

MAKES ABOUT 40

1 can (15½ ounces) black beans, drained and rinsed

2 small plum tomatoes, seeded and finely diced

1 ripe avocado, halved, pitted, peeled and diced

½ cup chopped fresh cilantro

2 tablespoons fresh lime juice

Salt and black pepper

Ground cumin, to taste

40 cup-shaped tortilla chips (such as Tostitos Scoops)

Fill these bites just before serving or the chips will get soggy. No need to worry about them wilting on the serving platter; they won't last that long.

1 In a medium bowl, combine all ingredients except chips. Season to taste.

2 Arrange tortilla chips on a platter. Using a small spoon, fill chip cups with bean mixture. Serve immediately.

TIP: Recipe calls for plum tomatoes because they are widely available year-round. Use whichever variety looks good in your market.

Mushroom and Caramelized Onion Tart

This savory tart is best served warm, but you can complete the recipe through step 2 up to 4 hours in advance. Top the crust with the veggies and bake just before serving.

SERVES 16

1 sheet frozen puff pastry, thawed according to package directions

1 tablespoon unsalted butter

1 carton (10 ounces) white mushrooms, trimmed and sliced

½ medium onion, thinly sliced

1 tablespoon chopped fresh oregano

Salt and black pepper

2 ounces soft goat cheese, crumbled

1. Preheat oven to 400°F. On a lightly floured surface, roll out thawed pastry to a 15-by-10-inch rectangle. Transfer to a baking sheet. Using the tines of a fork, score all around the perimeter of the dough to make a 1-inch border. Using points of the fork, prick all over the inside of the dough. Bake for 10 minutes, until golden. (Dough may puff up a bit.)

2. Meanwhile, melt butter in a medium nonstick skillet over medium heat. Add mushrooms and onion; cover and cook for 15 minutes, until tender and all the liquid has evaporated, stirring often. Reduce heat if onion is scorching. Stir in oregano, salt and pepper. Drain any liquid remaining in pan.

3. Spread mushroom mixture over crust. Sprinkle tart with goat cheese. Bake for 10 minutes, until crust is cooked through and cheese is lightly golden.

TIP: Sautéing mushrooms bring out their flavor. Just make sure you cook them in a hot pan with plenty of room for the juices to evaporate.

Cool Tzatziki Dip

MAKES 2 CUPS

1 large cucumber, peeled
and seeded

Salt and black pepper

½ small garlic clove, minced

2 tablespoons chopped
fresh mint

1 tablespoon fresh lemon juice

1 tablespoon extra-virgin olive oil

1 cup plain Greek yogurt

A fresh yogurt-and-cucumber dip is a healthy choice in this season of excess. Serve it cold with cut-up veggies and pita crisps.

1 Dice cucumber as finely as possible; place on a double-thick stack of paper towels. Lightly sprinkle cucumber with salt; let sit for 5 minutes to draw out moisture. Use paper towel to pat dry and blot moisture from cucumber.

2 In a medium bowl, combine chopped cucumber, garlic, mint, lemon juice and oil. Stir in yogurt. Season to taste with salt and pepper and additional lemon juice. Refrigerate for at least 1 hour.

TIP: Greek yogurt differs from conventional yogurt in that it has been strained to remove the whey. This process also removes excess water, resulting in thicker, creamier yogurt. It's perfect for concocting party dips.

Real Sour Cream and Onion Dip

Not for the faint of heart; this dip is super-rich and creamy. Serve at cool room temperature with chips and cut-up vegetables.

MAKES 2 CUPS

1. Warm butter and oil in a large nonstick skillet over medium-low heat. Add onions, cayenne, salt and pepper; cook for 10 minutes, stirring often. Reduce heat to low; cook for 20 minutes, until onions are a golden brown and caramelized, stirring often. Let cool.

2. Transfer onions to a food processor; pulse until chopped. Add cream cheese, sour cream and mayonnaise; pulse until blended. Season to taste with salt and pepper.

TIP: Cream cheese must be at room temperature in order to blend properly.

2 tablespoons unsalted butter

1 tablespoon olive oil

2 large onions, thinly sliced (about 3 cups)

¼ teaspoon cayenne pepper

Salt and black pepper

4 ounces (½ box) cream cheese, cut into chunks, at room temperature

¾ cup light or regular sour cream

¼ cup light or regular mayonnaise

Christmas Eve Eggnog

SERVES ABOUT 12

6 large eggs, separated

1 cup granulated sugar

3 cups whole milk

1 vanilla bean, split lengthwise

Salt

½ cup brandy

1 cup heavy cream

Garnishes: Ground nutmeg, chocolate shavings, cinnamon sticks

This classic eggnog recipe calls for warming the egg yolks to assure a decadent, delicious yet safe drink for your party guests. (Except, of course, for children!)

1. Place a large bowl in a larger bowl of ice water; set aside.

2. In a medium bowl, whisk egg yolks and ½ cup of the sugar until thick, for about 2 minutes.

3. In a medium saucepan over medium-low heat, bring milk, vanilla bean, and pinch salt to a simmer. Remove from heat; whisk 1 cup of this hot milk mixture into the yolks. Slowly pour yolk-milk mixture into milk remaining in saucepan. Place pan over medium heat; cook, stirring constantly with a wooden spoon, until mixture reaches 160°F and is thick enough to coat the back of spoon.

4. Strain eggnog base through a fine-mesh sieve into bowl in ice bath. Let cool for about 20 minutes, stirring occasionally. Cover and refrigerate until chilled, for about 1 hour.

5. Whisk brandy and cream into chilled eggnog. In large bowl using an electric mixer on high speed, beat egg whites until soft peaks form. Add remaining ½ cup sugar; beat on high until stiff peaks form. Gently fold whites into eggnog until blended. Cover, refrigerate for several hours or overnight, or until cold. Pour into a pitcher to serve. Garnish servings as desired.

TIP: Vanilla beans are the dried seedpods of the vanilla plant. To use, slice the long pods open lengthwise to expose the tiny seeds inside.

The Holiday Table

This season, dress up your holiday meal with these simple and lovely ideas.

For a fun, whimsical setting, use a variety of Christmas tableware. Throughout the year, collect vintage Christmas plates, platters and bowls at tag sales or online auctions. Set your table with all of them at once.

You can never have too many candles. Nestle candles of all sizes into glass or pottery pedestals or cake platters. For the most elegant look, purchase candles all in the same color. For an added holiday touch, draw designs on the candles with metallic pens (such as Sharpies) or tie holiday ribbons around each candle.

Add sparkle with glittering candles. How to: In a large cardboard box, place a few candles and lightly coat with spray adhesive (find it at craft stores). Gently spoon fine glitter over the candles; remove to a wire rack and let dry overnight.

Silver accents add luster to the table. Line a large silver bowl with evergreen boughs and juniper branches (with blue berries attached). Lightly coat small pinecones or hemlock cones with silver metallic spray; nestle these among the branches, along with small silver tree ornaments.

Where Shall I Sit?

Personalize table settings with creative ideas for homemade place cards for your holiday celebrations.

Make a tiny, take-home Christmas tree for each dinner guest. For each tree, cut a thick branch into thin rounds with flat bottoms. Using a sharp point, poke a hole in the center of each base. Insert small evergreen sprigs into holes. Nestle a small name tag in the branches, or use as a star to top the tree.

Personalized Christmas ornaments add a splash of fun to the table. Buy several small ornaments that match your table linens. Using metallic pens, write guests' names on ornaments and rest them against wine glasses.

Make a sweet first impression with small-fruit place cards. The stems of seckel (a miniature variety) pears or lady apples can hold paper name tags punched with holes and tied in place with ribbon. Other place holders: clementines (use whole cloves to attach the tag), sweetgum seeds and jack-be-little pumpkins.

Tuck holiday greenery nosegays into napkin rings. Bind small pine boughs (or fresh rosemary branches) together with raffia into a small bouquet. Write guests' names on a small piece of cardstock punched with a hole. Using colored twine or embroidery thread, tie name tag to bouquet.

Use glowing votive candles to direct guests to their seats. Cut a piece of vellum or parchment paper to completely wrap around a small votive holder. Write guests' names on paper. Wrap paper around votive, and secure with double-sided tape. Remember to write guests' names on both sides of the candle, so that others can read the names from across the table.

Christmas and Christmas Eve Dinner

I grew up with the traditional Christmas dinner—turkey, two kinds of stuffing (rice and bread), mashed potatoes, gelatin salads plus enough side dishes to cover most of the table. Naturally, there was an abundance of family—uncles, aunts and cousins—too. We had two or three card tables, called the Kids' Tables, positioned in different areas of the house.

After Wayne and I were married and had children, it soon became apparent that our Christmases would be quite different. For several years, I did try to re-create the traditional Christmas meal. First thing Christmas morning, the turkey went into the oven and I cooked and baked and spent hour after hour in the kitchen. I wanted to share with my husband and family the Christmases I'd known as a child.

To my disappointment no one really cared. The kids just wanted to play with their new toys; they weren't interested in trying Grandma Adler's special rice dressing. Wayne was busy assembling bikes and toys, and my big dinner was more of a distraction than a pleasure.

As a result, I decided we needed to do something different. So I created our own new approach to Christmas dinner, one that involved very little work on my part on Christmas Day.

On Christmas Eve, I asked Wayne and each of the children to choose their favorite dish. Ted loved my layered salad, Jenny Adele wanted my special bread salad with real crab, Dale liked chicken wings best and Jody chose an ice cream dessert made with crumbled cookies. Wayne wanted potato salad, exactly like the kind my dad loved so much. Everything was prepared in advance, so all I had to do was set it out on the table, buffet style. That way everyone could eat what they wanted, when they wanted. (Certain favorites changed over the years, of course.)

Shortly after I started my buffet-style Christmas meals, I happened to pick up a jigsaw puzzle. It became a family tradition to put together a jigsaw every Christmas—a big one. We'd finish it that day. At some point we'd all gravitate toward it, singly or in groups, add a section or a piece and then drift away. Wayne was the most dedicated to getting the puzzle completed before midnight.

Much later, as our children married and had families of their own, and Wayne and I headed for Florida during Christmas week, there were further changes. We now do a Progressive Family Dinner the weekend before Christmas. Ted and Lana and their two children live the farthest away, so we start at their home with the soup course. Jenny Adele and Kevin provide the appetizers, and Dale and Laurie serve the salads. The main course is at our house and then we end the day with desserts, which Jody brings over.

As you can imagine, this takes quite a few hours. A Progressive Dinner gives each family the opportunity to show off their home, all decorated for Christmas. After every course, the host family passes around the gifts they have for the grandchildren. In the kids' eyes that makes it a truly exciting event.

After dessert we gather for several rounds of bingo. Years ago my father obtained used bingo cards and equipment from the Yakima VFW, of which he was a member. They were about to toss them, but Dad laid claim to them instead. We've played bingo every Christmas since then. (The kids have continued the Christmas Day jigsaw tradition in their own homes.) The prizes are usually gift cards or lotto scratch tickets. Wayne calls out the numbers with a lot of flair and the grandkids each get a chance to turn the cage. There's a special gift for whichever family is the ultimate winner.

This is old-fashioned family fun and everyone has a great time. Naturally there are goodies to munch on—mostly popcorn, plus homemade cookies and candy.

In *The Perfect Christmas*, Cassie has to prepare a wonderful Christmas dinner for her neighbors as one of the tasks she must perform before the matchmaker deems her worthy of meeting her perfect mate. Like me as a young bride, she struggles to make everything as *perfect* as a magazine photograph . . . with hilarious results. I believe this is a rite of passage every woman probably faces at some time or other.

Whatever you decide to do for *your* Christmas dinner or family celebration, I hope you'll enjoy it as much as my family enjoys ours. And I hope you'll find some ideas in this chapter—and in the rest of this book.

Cider-Glazed Roast Turkey

SERVES 12

2½ cups apple cider

¼ cup Calvados or applejack brandy

6 tablespoons (¾ stick) unsalted butter, cut into chunks and at room temperature

2 tablespoons chopped fresh thyme, plus 8 sprigs for garnish

1 14-pound turkey, with giblets, rinsed

Salt and black pepper

4 tart apples, each peeled, cored and cut into 8 slices

1 medium onion, chopped

2 celery stalks, chopped

4 fresh sage leaves

½ teaspoon ground cinnamon

GRAVY

1 can (14½ ounces) reduced-sodium chicken broth, as needed

½ cup apple cider

2 tablespoons cornstarch

TIP: If you are stuffing the turkey with a different dressing, scatter the apple mixture all around the turkey in the roasting pan.

A generous slathering of spiked cider butter makes for a beautiful golden roast. Instructions here are for a 14-pound bird; adapt cooking times to the size of your turkey. As always, use a meat thermometer to check for doneness.

1. In a small saucepan over medium heat, bring ½ cup of the cider and Calvados just to a boil. Lower heat; simmer for 2 minutes, until reduced by half. Remove from heat; stir in butter and chopped thyme. Freeze for 30 minutes, or until solid.

2. Preheat to 400°F; position a rack in the lower third of the oven. Rinse turkey inside and out; pat dry with paper towels. Sprinkle cavity with salt and pepper. Using your fingers, gently loosen skin from breast and spread about half of the maple butter over breast meat under the skin. Rub the remaining maple butter all over outside of turkey. Place turkey on a rack in a large, heavy roasting pan. Season with salt and pepper.

3. In a large bowl, toss half of the sliced apples, onion, celery, sage, cinnamon, salt and pepper until combined. Fill turkey cavity with as much of the mixture as possible. Tuck wing tips under turkey; tie legs together loosely. Place turkey in large roasting pan. Scatter remaining apple mixture and turkey giblets and neck around turkey. Pour remaining 2 cups cider into pan.

4. Place turkey in oven; reduce temperature to 350°F. Roast for about 3 hours, basting often with the pan juices, until an instant-read thermometer inserted in the thickest part of the thigh without touching the bone registers 165°F. Cover turkey loosely with foil to keep from browning too quickly during cooking, if necessary. Transfer turkey to platter; tent loosely with foil and let rest for 20 minutes (internal temperature of turkey will increase while standing).

5. For gravy: Using a slotted spoon, transfer apples from roasting pan to a bowl. Strain pan drippings into a large glass measuring cup; discard solids in the strainer. Skim off any fat from drippings. Add enough broth to pan juices to measure 4 cups. Transfer broth mixture to large saucepan over medium-high heat. Bring to a simmer; let cook for 5 minutes. Add reserved apple slices; simmer for 2 minutes. In a small bowl, whisk cider and cornstarch. Whisk into gravy, still over medium-high heat. Simmer for 2 minutes, until gravy thickens. Season with salt and pepper. Discard stuffing from turkey cavity before carving.

Savory Herb-Roasted Chicken

SERVES 8

6 tablespoons (¾ stick) unsalted butter, at room temperature

2 tablespoons chopped fresh parsley plus 6 large sprigs

2 tablespoons chopped fresh thyme plus 6 large sprigs

2 tablespoons chopped fresh rosemary plus 6 small sprigs

Salt and black pepper

2 whole chickens (3½ to 4 pounds each), rinsed and patted dry

1 lemon, quartered

8 garlic cloves, smashed

As with all roasts, it's important to give it some resting time before carving. This allows the juices to retreat back into the flesh.

1. In a medium bowl, combine butter, all chopped herbs, and about ½ teaspoon salt; stir until blended.

2. Preheat oven to 375°F; set rack in bottom third of oven. Season inside cavity of chickens with salt and pepper; stuff with lemon slices, smashed garlic and herb sprigs. Starting at neck end, slide fingers under skin of breast and upper part of legs, loosening skin on each chicken. For each bird, scoop up about 2 tablespoons of the herb butter and spread under skin on breast and upper leg meat. Place chickens, breast-side up, on racks in a large roasting pan; tie legs together loosely to hold shape. Spread top and sides of chickens with remaining herb butter; sprinkle with salt and pepper.

3. Roast about 1½ hours, occasionally basting birds with pan juices. Chicken is done when an instant-read thermometer inserted in the thickest part of the thigh without touching the bone registers 165°F. Transfer chickens to a board; let rest for 10 minutes before carving.

TIP: Chicken can be prepped and stuffed up to 1 day ahead. Cover bird and refrigerate. Bring to room temperature before continuing recipe.

Mom's Rice Stuffing with Water Chestnuts, Apples and Hazelnuts

Mom served this rice dish every Thanksgiving and Christmas. The recipe was handed down by her mother, who emigrated from the Black Sea region of Ukraine as a young married woman in the late 1800s. Until now, it's never been written down, but passed from one daughter to the next.

1. Melt butter in heavy large pot over medium heat. Add onion, celery and thyme; cook for 6 minutes, stirring often. Add rice and broth; bring to a simmer. Reduce heat to low; cover and cook for 22 minutes, without stirring, until liquid is absorbed and rice is just tender. Stir in water chestnuts, apples, hazelnuts, scallions, raisins and parsley. Season with salt and pepper.

2. If stuffing turkey: Loosely fill cavity with dressing. Place any leftover dressing in a buttered casserole. Cover dish with buttered foil, buttered-side down. Bake dressing for 30 minutes at 350°F, or until heated through.

3. If not stuffing turkey: Preheat oven to 350°F. Butter a 15-by-10-inch glass or ceramic baking dish. Stir ½ cup turkey drippings into dressing; spoon into prepared dish. Cover dish with buttered foil, buttered-side down. Bake dressing for 40 minutes, or until heated through.

TIP: Save time and hassle by using prepeeled and chopped hazelnuts. Find them in the baking section of your market.

SERVES 12 TO 16

6 tablespoons (¾ stick) unsalted butter

1 large onion, finely chopped

2 celery stalks, thinly sliced

2 tablespoons chopped fresh thyme

2½ cups white rice

5 cups reduced-sodium chicken broth

1 can (8 ounces) water chestnuts, drained and chopped (about 1 cup)

2 tart apples, peeled and chopped

1½ cups hazelnuts, toasted, peeled and coarsely chopped

4 scallions, thinly sliced

1 cup raisins

½ cup chopped fresh parsley

Salt and black pepper

Classic Bread Stuffing with Leeks and Bacon

SERVES 8

½ pound apple-smoked bacon, sliced

4 tablespoons (½ stick) unsalted butter, chopped

4 celery stalks, thinly sliced

4 carrots, peeled and thinly sliced

3 leeks, thinly sliced and rinsed

1 tablespoon chopped fresh thyme

2 teaspoons chopped fresh sage

Salt and black pepper

1 bag (1 pound) packaged bread-stuffing mix (plain or seasoned)

1 cup chopped pecans

¾ cup chopped fresh parsley

3 cups reduced-sodium chicken broth

Every cook needs a good basic bread stuffing in his or her repertoire. This one fits the bill.

1. Cook bacon in a Dutch oven or large heavy skillet over medium heat until crisp. Transfer to a paper-towel-lined plate to drain; crumble. Drain and discard all but 2 tablespoons of the drippings in pan.

2. In same pot over medium-low heat, melt 2 tablespoons of the butter with the remaining bacon fat. Add celery, carrots, leeks, thyme, sage, salt and pepper. Cook for 12 minutes, stirring often. Transfer to a large bowl. Fold in bread cubes, pecans, parsley and bacon crumbles. Slowly pour in broth; folding in liquid until bread cubes are evenly moistened.

3. If stuffing turkey: Let mixture cool completely. Loosely fill turkey with stuffing. Place any leftover stuffing in a buttered casserole; top with remaining 2 tablespoons chopped butter. Bake as directed in step 4.

4. If not stuffing turkey: Spoon mixture into a large buttered casserole or roasting pan. Top with remaining chopped butter. Bake in a preheated 400°F oven for 35 minutes, or until warmed through.

TIP: Although any bacon will do, apple-smoked varieties are especially good.

Three-Cheese Scalloped Potatoes

This is a great dish for entertaining because it can be made entirely in advance, the morning of your party. Cover and store at room temperature—heat up the casserole before serving.

SERVES 8 TO 10

1. Preheat oven to 350°F. Combine all cheeses in a medium bowl.

2. Melt butter in large Dutch oven or deep skillet over medium-high heat. Add onion; cook for 4 minutes, until softened, stirring. Add garlic, salt and pepper; cook for 30 seconds, stirring. Gradually pour in milk; bring just to a simmer. Reduce heat; cook for 3 minutes, until slightly thickened and hot but not scalded. Sprinkle in nutmeg.

3. Meanwhile, butter bottom of a 9-by-13-inch nonreactive baking pan. Layer half of the potato slices in pan. Pour half of the warm milk and sprinkle half of the cheese over potatoes. Top with remaining potatoes and remaining warm milk. (Milk will not cover potatoes completely.) Reserve remaining cheese.

4. Cover baking dish tightly with foil; bake for 45 minutes. Uncover dish (liquids in dish may look curdled); sprinkle potatoes with reserved cheese mixture. Bake for 45 minutes, uncovered, until potatoes are tender and cheese is golden brown. Remove from oven; let stand for 10 minutes before serving.

1 cup shredded extra-sharp cheddar cheese

¾ cup shredded Gruyère or Jarlsberg cheese

½ cup freshly grated Parmesan

2 tablespoons unsalted butter, plus extra for pan

½ medium onion, finely chopped

2 garlic cloves, minced

Salt and black pepper

3 cups whole milk

½ teaspoon ground nutmeg

3¾ to 4 pounds russet potatoes, peeled and cut into ⅛-inch-thick rounds

TIP: Slicing strategy for slippery potatoes: Cut a thin slice from the long end of each potato to make a flat bottom. Set this bottom on your cutting board to keep the potato in place while you slice.

Mashed Potatoes with Roasted Garlic

SERVES 8

2 whole heads garlic

2 teaspoons olive oil

Salt and black pepper

5 pounds Yukon Gold potatoes, peeled and coarsely chopped

½ cup unsalted butter, cut into chunks

8 ounces (1 box) cream cheese, cut into chunks, at room temperature

½ cup whole milk or half-and-half

Snipped fresh chives, for garnish

Roasted garlic adds a sweet and nutty flavor to creamy mashed potatoes. This dish can be made up to 4 hours in advance. Cover tightly and store at room temperature. Warm in the oven or microwave.

1 Preheat oven to 350°F. Slice off the top quarter of each garlic head. Drizzle about 1 teaspoon oil over the cut side of each head; sprinkle with salt. Wrap each head in foil; place on a baking sheet. Bake for about 45 minutes, until cloves are soft when squeezed. Unwrap garlic; let sit until cool enough to handle.

2 Place potatoes in a large saucepot; cover with water by at least 2 inches. Bring to a boil over high heat. Cook for 15 minutes, or until potatoes are very tender. Drain.

3 Return potatoes to pot; set over low heat. Hold roasted garlic heads over potatoes, cut-side down. Squeeze heads to release garlic puree into potatoes. Using a potato masher, mash to combine. Add butter, cream cheese and milk; mash to desired consistency. Season to taste with salt and pepper. Garnish with chives.

TIP: The easiest, cleanest way to chop chives is to hold a bunch in your hand and use scissors to snip the long strands into tiny bits.

Creamed Spinach and Feta Pie

Don't worry about making the pastry look perfect; when it bakes, it puffs and turns into a burnished golden frame.

SERVES 8 TO 10

1. Preheat oven to 375°F. Lightly brush bottom and sides of an 8-inch springform pan with some of the melted butter. On a lightly floured surface, roll out 1 thawed pastry sheet to about ⅛-inch thick, attempting to make the sheet as square as possible. Fit pastry sheet into pan, pressing dough into pan edges and carefully bringing pastry edges to hang over top of the pan. (Don't worry if all sides of pan aren't completely covered with pastry.)

2. Warm oil in a large heavy skillet over medium-low heat. Add onion, salt and pepper; cook for 8 minutes, until onion is softened, stirring often.

3. Place spinach in a colander set in sink; press down to extract as much liquid as possible. In a large bowl, whisk eggs and nutmeg until blended. Fold in drained spinach, ¾ cup of the Parmesan, feta and bread crumbs. Spoon spinach mixture into the prepared crust.

4. Roll out remaining sheet of thawed pastry to a ⅛-inch-thick square. Place sheet on top of the filling. Arrange points of top pastry square to slide down and cover any bare spots in pan. Fold any excess pastry under itself so that it forms a ridge around pan edges. Brush top and ridge of pastry with remaining melted butter; sprinkle pie with remaining Parmesan.

5. Place pie on a rimmed baking sheet and bake for 1 hour, until top is golden and filling is cooked through and hot.

TIP: Make sure to press out as much liquid as possible from the spinach, or the dish will be watery.

Ingredients

- 2 tablespoons unsalted butter, melted
- 2 sheets frozen puff pastry, thawed
- 2 tablespoons olive oil
- 1 large onion, finely chopped
- Salt and black pepper
- 3 packages (10-ounce size) frozen chopped spinach, thawed and coarsely chopped
- 6 large eggs
- 1 teaspoon ground nutmeg
- ¾ cup plus ¼ cup grated Parmesan cheese
- 8 ounces feta cheese, cut into small dice
- ¼ cup plain bread crumbs

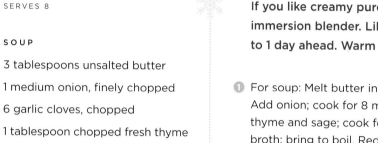

Butternut Squash Bisque with Jarlsberg Toasts

SERVES 8

SOUP

3 tablespoons unsalted butter

1 medium onion, finely chopped

6 garlic cloves, chopped

1 tablespoon chopped fresh thyme

2 teaspoons chopped fresh sage

1 medium (about 2½ pounds) butternut squash, peeled and cut into 1-inch chunks

5 cups (40 ounces) reduced-sodium chicken broth

1 tablespoon sherry or red-wine vinegar

2 tablespoons heavy cream

Salt and black pepper

GARNISH

8 thin baguette slices

Olive oil, for drizzling

½ cup shredded Jarlsberg cheese

Chopped fresh thyme

Salt

If you like creamy pureed soups, you might want to invest in an immersion blender. Like most winter soups, this one can be made up to 1 day ahead. Warm over medium-low heat before serving.

1. For soup: Melt butter in a large heavy pot over medium-low heat. Add onion; cook for 8 minutes, until softened, stirring often. Add garlic, thyme and sage; cook for 1 minute, stirring. Add squash cubes and broth; bring to boil. Reduce heat, cover and simmer for 20 minutes, until squash is very tender.

2. Using a blender (or an immersion blender), puree soup until smooth. Return soup to same pot. Stir in vinegar and cream; simmer until warmed through. Season with salt and pepper.

3. For toasts: Preheat broiler. Arrange bread slices on a baking sheet. Lightly drizzle slices with oil. Broil for 1 minute, until golden. Flip; sprinkle evenly with cheese, thyme and salt. Broil for 1 minute, until cheese melts. Ladle soup into bowls. Float 1 toast in each bowl.

TIP: Hard winter squashes can be tricky to cut. One way to make it easier: Prick squash in a few places with a knife; microwave for about 3 minutes. The skin should soften.

Slow-Roasted Provençal Tomatoes

SERVES 10 TO 12

⅓ cup plain bread crumbs

½ cup chopped fresh
Italian parsley

2 teaspoons chopped
fresh thyme

4 garlic cloves, minced

¼ cup olive oil

8 medium tomatoes, halved
horizontally

Salt

If you want to add a new flavor to your holiday meal, try this simple yet spectacular warm tomato dish.

1. Preheat oven to 400°F. In a medium bowl, toss bread crumbs, parsley, thyme and garlic until combined.

2. Warm oil in a large skillet over medium-high heat. Place 4 tomato halves, cut-side down, on hot skillet. Sear for 4 minutes, until browned. Transfer to a large roasting pan, browned-side up. Repeat with remaining tomatoes. Pour juices in skillet over tomatoes in roasting pan.

3. Evenly sprinkle tomatoes with herb mixture; season with salt. Bake for 30 minutes, until soft and sizzling. Serve warm.

> **TIP:** Even the blandest of winter tomatoes taste good when cooked this way. Although you may substitute dried thyme for fresh, stick with fresh parsley; the dried variety is dull and flavorless.

Old-Fashioned Oyster Stew with Fennel

Although this rich stew is a great first course for your Christmas dinner, it also makes a filling main course when served with hot rolls and a green salad.

SERVES 6 AS A FIRST COURSE;
4 AS A MAIN COURSE

① Generously butter a nonreactive skillet; arrange oysters in a single layer in skillet.

② In a small saucepan over medium heat, combine shallots, wine and 1 tablespoon of the butter. Bring to a boil; reduce heat and simmer for 10 minutes, until reduced by half.

③ Strain reserved oyster liquid through a fine-mesh sieve, and add to reduced wine mixture. Return to a boil; pour this hot mixture over oysters in skillet. Set skillet over medium heat. Cook for 30 seconds. Using tongs, flip oysters and cook for 2 minutes. Using a slotted spoon, transfer oysters to a large plate. Reserve the oyster cooking liquid.

④ Melt 5 tablespoons of the butter in a medium saucepan over medium heat. Add onion and fennel; cook for 4 minutes, until softened. Whisk in the reserved oyster cooking liquid, the cream and curry, and cook for 6 minutes, until sauce is reduced. Whisk in the remaining 2 tablespoons of butter. Add oysters; cook for 1 minute, until just warmed through.

⑤ Ladle hot soup into shallow soup bowls. Garnish with chives.

24 (about 1½ pints) freshly shucked oysters, with liquid reserved

3 shallots, finely chopped

1⅔ cups dry white wine, preferably chardonnay

8 tablespoons (1 stick) cold unsalted butter, plus more for pan

1 medium onion, finely chopped

1 small fennel bulb, halved, cored and finely chopped

1 cup heavy cream

Pinch curry powder

¼ cup snipped fresh chives

TIP: You'll need a fine mesh sieve for straining the oyster liquid, to make sure you strain out any sand. For presentation sake, trim the dark ruffled beards from the oysters using scissors.

Endive and Radicchio Christmas Salad

SERVES 8

¾ cup slivered almonds

5 tablespoons extra-virgin
olive oil

3 tablespoons white-wine vinegar

1 tablespoon fresh lemon juice

Salt and black pepper

3 medium Belgian endive,
trimmed, halved crosswise and
thinly sliced lengthwise

1 large radicchio head
(10 ounces), halved, cored
and thinly sliced lengthwise

2 Fuji or Gala apples, unpeeled
and thinly sliced

The vibrant colors of this salad mimic the red-and-green colors of the season. Although these are firmer greens than most, like any other salad, remember to toss with dressing just before serving.

1 Preheat oven to 300°F. Spread nuts on a baking sheet; bake for 5 minutes, until toasted and golden, stirring often. Cool.

2 In a large serving bowl, whisk oil, vinegar, juice, salt and pepper until blended. Add endive, radicchio, apples and nuts; toss to combine.

TIP: When making salad dressings, or any uncooked dish, it's best to use intensely flavored extra-virgin olive oil.

Shown on page 210.

Crisp Green Layered Salad

Serve this crunchy salad in a glass bowl to show off the colorful layers. Get a head start on your meal by making this a day in advance; it's just as good the next day. Remember to wait to toss the layers with the dressing just before serving.

1. For dressing: In a medium bowl, whisk mayonnaise and sour cream until blended.

2. Cook bacon in a large heavy skillet over medium heat until crisp. Transfer to paper-towel–lined plate to drain; crumble. In a medium saucepan, cook eggs until hard-boiled. Cool, peel and chop.

3. For salad: Add half of the lettuce to the bottom of a large glass bowl. Top with a layer of chopped eggs, peas, celery, the remaining lettuce, crumbled bacon, scallions and cheese. Spread dressing over top, smoothing to cover salad completely.

4. Cover salad tightly with plastic wrap. Refrigerate for at least 1 hour, or up to 24 hours. Toss dressing with salad just before serving. Add salt and pepper to taste.

TIP: Depending on the diameter of your bowl, you may need to increase the topping amounts to completely cover the salad.

SERVES 8 TO 10

DRESSING

½ cup mayonnaise

½ cup sour cream

SALAD

¾ pound sliced bacon

5 large eggs

1 head romaine lettuce, chopped (about 8 cups)

1 package (10 ounces) frozen peas, thawed

2 celery stalks, sliced

5 scallions, sliced

1½ cups shredded Swiss or cheddar cheese

Salt and black pepper

Winter Pear, Walnut and Baby Romaine Salad with Creamy Maple Vinaigrette

SERVES 8

VINAIGRETTE

2 tablespoons heavy cream or half-and-half

2 tablespoons pure maple syrup

3 tablespoons white balsamic or other white-wine vinegar

⅓ cup extra-virgin olive oil

Salt and black pepper

SALAD

2 boxes (5-ounce size) baby romaine or spring greens (about 20 cups lightly packed)

3 firm-ripe pears, cut into matchstick-size strips

1 cup dried cranberries

1 cup toasted, chopped walnuts

½ cup crumbled blue cheese or goat cheese

This is no everyday salad—it's alive with color, flavor and texture. If the sharp flavor of blue cheese is not to your liking, substitute milder goat cheese.

① For vinaigrette: In a large serving bowl, whisk cream, syrup and vinegar until blended. Gradually whisk in oil until mixture thickens. Season to taste with salt and pepper.

② For salad: Add greens, pears, cranberries and nuts to bowl. Toss to coat with vinaigrette. Garnish with cheese.

TIP: The dressing can be prepared up to 3 days ahead. Cover and refrigerate. Slice the pears and toss the salad with the vinaigrette just before serving.

Goodies to Go

A little creativity goes a long way; some easy ideas for pretty presentation and safe transport of your holiday gifts.

Gift baskets don't need to be purchased at the store; look for them all year long at tag sales and thrift shops. Furthermore, ribbons need not be red and green—select color combinations you think your recipient will like.

Give new life to packaging used for other products, such as cookie tins, cardboard oatmeal containers, old jewelry boxes or cigar boxes. More ideas: terra-cotta pots, squat flower vases, old-time apothecary jars, vintage pottery bowls, canvas tote bags, reusable shopping bags.

Keep fragile gifts safe by wrapping them in holiday kitchen towels or napkins. Instead of packaging peanuts, use real peanuts or walnuts and pecans, still in their shells. Run scraps of last year's wrapping paper through a paper shredder and use that to cushion packages or in place of tissue paper in holiday gift bags.

Create festive cones for hand-delivered treats. To make: Using a compass opened as wide as possible, draw an arc onto a sheet of construction paper or cardstock. Cut along the line with pinking shears. Roll the paper into a cone and use a glue gun or staple to hold the shape. Decorate cones with rick-rack, ribbons or beads. Punch holes to string a ribbon handle through; knot the ends. Fill with gifts.

Give a cardboard candy or jewelry box a merry makeover by covering the top of the lid with colorful wrapping paper, pretty fabric or a Christmas card. Using a ruler, draw an outline that's about ½ inch larger than the lid on the paper. Cut along the line with pinking shears. Glue the cutout to the lid; pressing the paper on top and down the sides of the lid.

Wrap It Up!

These festive presentations will assure your gift is the first to be opened on Christmas morning.

Think way beyond commercial wrapping paper. Some options for wrapping you might even have on hand: kids' artwork, fabric, maps, restaurant menus, comic or sports pages, foreign newspapers, sewing patterns. More good news: reusing papers is better for the environment, since most wrapping paper can't be recycled.

Go natural and wrap gifts in brown butcher paper or brown grocery bags. Continue the theme with a raffia ribbon and tiny sprig of holly or pine.

For a cooking friend, cover presents in wax or parchment paper; tie with baker's twine and a tiny kitchen-themed tree ornament.

Homemade gift tags lend a personal touch. Outline the shapes of small holiday cookie cutters onto colored construction paper or cardstock. Carefully cut out the designs with an X-ACTO knife and write the recipient's name on the tag. Punch a hole in the top and string with ribbon.

For an extra-special treat, add an embellishment or present-topper to each gift. Use your imagination and add something you know the recipient will love: a vintage clip earring, a tiny tree ornament, red-and-white pipe cleaners twisted together and formed into a candy cane shape.

Christmas Desserts

I have a confession to make: I have a notorious sweet tooth. I come by this honestly, since both my father and Grandpa Adler had the same addiction. I'm not the only one in the family who inherited this, either. Several of my cousins have sweet cravings, too, so you can picture what it's like at family events. We don't dare suggest a potluck because there'd be seven desserts to every entrée or side dish.

Growing up in Yakima, Washington, I was surrounded by family. Not a holiday passed without a huge gathering of cousins, uncles and aunts. Some of my fondest childhood memories are of spending Christmas Eve with my cousins following Midnight Mass. We traveled to one another's homes, opened gifts and didn't get to bed until two or three in the morning. Very exciting for a child. Then on Christmas morning my brother and I slept in late and woke to the scent of pies baking or a turkey roasting. Mom would be working in the kitchen; she'd ask my father, brother or me to taste her stuffing to make sure it had just the right mixture of herbs and spices. I don't think any of us ever refused.

I don't really consider a meal complete if it doesn't end with something sweet or gooey and yummy. For holiday dinners such as Thanksgiving and Christmas, my family generally has four or five different dessert options from which to choose. For instance, the pies, of which I invariably make several. Pumpkin and pecan, apple and pear are some of my favorites. There are any number of ways to jazz those up. In years past, especially when the children were younger, I'd bake a birthday cake for dessert on Christmas Day; after all, Christmas is the celebration of Christ's birth, which is the whole point, isn't it?

Who among us can limit ourselves to just one dessert on such a festive occasion? Truth be known, it isn't uncommon for me to taste a small bit of each.

My love of sweets is one of the reasons I decided Heavenly Delights, the restaurant mentioned in *Call Me Mrs. Miracle,* should specialize in desserts. And since the story takes place in New York City, it only makes sense that Lucie's going to have cheesecake on the menu. (There are a couple of really terrific ones in this chapter!)

The idea for the character of Mrs. Miracle was generated by the Book of Hebrews, Chapter 13, where it says that we shouldn't forget to entertain strangers for some have entertained angels unaware. Hmm . . . angels unaware? Just like Shirley, Goodness and Mercy (who are some of my most popular characters), Emily Merkle arrived full-blown in my mind, an angel who visits those most in need during the holiday season.

I'm thrilled that Hallmark Channel chose to produce two movies using the character of Mrs. Miracle, played by Doris Roberts. (I now picture Doris when I'm writing about Mrs. Miracle!)

I'm sure Emily Merkle, aka Mrs. Miracle, would agree that it wouldn't feel like Christmas without dessert. Few of us are willing to diet during the holidays, and with good reason. That's when the very best desserts come from our kitchens, and those of our family and friends.

Ginger Pear Crumble

SERVES 8

CRUST

8 ounces gingersnap cookies

3 tablespoons granulated sugar

6 tablespoons (¾ stick) unsalted butter, melted

FILLING

3 pounds ripe Anjou or Bosc pears (about 5), peeled, cored and chopped

¼ cup granulated sugar

2 tablespoons all-purpose flour

1 teaspoon ground cinnamon

½ teaspoon ground ginger

TOPPING

1 cup all-purpose flour

⅓ cup brown sugar

5 tablespoons unsalted butter, at room temperature

Pinch salt

This is one of those desserts that's best eaten the day it's baked. Serve it warm with vanilla ice cream.

1. For crust: Preheat oven to 375°F. Position a rack in lower third of oven. In a food processor, pulse cookies with sugar into fine crumbs. Add melted butter; pulse until crumbs are moist and hold together when squeezed. Press crumbs in bottom and up sides of a 9-inch pie tin.

2. For filling: In a large bowl, toss pears, sugar, flour, cinnamon and ginger. Spoon fruit into prepared crust.

3. For topping: In a large bowl with electric mixer on medium speed, combine flour, brown sugar, butter and salt. Beat until crumbs form. Crumbs should hold together when squeezed.

4. Sprinkle topping evenly over pear filling. Place pie on a baking sheet and bake for 50 minutes, until topping is golden brown and fruit is tender and bubbling.

TIP: No ripe pears at the market? Use tart apples instead.

Chocolate Cream Tart with Raspberries

This dessert looks prettiest in a ridged tart pan, but you could also use a regular pie tin.

SERVES 8 TO 10

CRUST

9 tablespoons (1 stick plus 1 tablespoon) unsalted butter, chopped and at room temperature

½ cup confectioners' sugar

1 egg yolk

1½ cups all-purpose flour

1 tablespoon heavy cream

FILLING

8 ounces semisweet chocolate, chips or finely chopped

4 tablespoons (½ stick) unsalted butter, cut into chunks

3 large eggs, separated

4 tablespoons granulated sugar

1 cup cold heavy cream

2 containers (6-ounce size) fresh raspberries

Confectioners' sugar, for garnish

1. For crust: In a large bowl with electric mixer on medium speed, beat butter and confectioners' sugar until blended. Add egg yolk; beat until incorporated. Add flour and cream; beat until combined. Form dough into a disk; wrap in plastic. Refrigerate until firm, for at least 1 hour or up to 2 days.

2. Preheat oven to 375°F. Butter a 9-inch ridged tart pan with removable bottom. Remove dough from refrigerator; let sit for 15 minutes until softened. Roll out dough on lightly floured surface to a 12-inch round. Place dough in pan; pressing dough into bottom and sides to fit snugly. Fold any overhanging dough under itself against pan sides to strengthen crust. Freeze for 20 minutes. Using a fork, poke a few holes in the crust. Bake crust for 20 to 25 minutes, until golden. Transfer to a wire rack to cool.

3. For filling: Melt chocolate and butter in a bowl set over a saucepan of hot water, stirring often. Remove from heat; stir until smooth. Place bowl back over heat; beat in egg yolks.

4. In a large bowl with electric mixer on high speed, beat egg whites until soft peaks form. Add 2 tablespoons of the sugar; beat until stiff. Fold egg whites into chocolate mixture until blended. Wipe out mixing bowl.

5. In a large bowl with electric mixer on high speed, beat cream until frothy. Add remaining 2 tablespoons sugar; beat until soft peaks form. Gently fold chocolate mixture into the cream until blended.

6. Spoon chocolate cream into cooled pie shell. Arrange raspberries decoratively on top of it. Refrigerate until cold. Sprinkle tart with confectioners' sugar just before serving.

TIP: The crust dough can be made up to 2 days in advance; however, the tart is best served the day it's baked.

White Chocolate Peppermint Cheesecake

SERVES 16

CRUST

10 ounces mint-flavored chocolate sandwich cookies (about 25 cookies)

4 tablespoons (½ stick) unsalted butter, melted

FILLING

4 packages (8-ounce size) cream cheese, at room temperature

1⅓ cups granulated sugar

2 tablespoons all-purpose flour

2 teaspoons vanilla extract

4 large eggs

2 tablespoons sour cream

GLAZE

2 ounces white chocolate, chopped, or white chocolate chips

1 tablespoon unsalted butter

¾ cup confectioners' sugar

2 tablespoons half-and-half or heavy cream

Peppermint patty candies, for garnish

This super-rich, mile-high cheesecake will feed a crowd. Be careful, the batter fills the pan to the very top.

① For crust: Preheat oven to 350°F. Position a rack in center of oven. Wrap foil around outside and up sides of a 9-inch springform pan. In a food processor, pulse cookies into fine crumbs. Add melted butter; process until crumbs are moist and hold together when squeezed. Press crumbs into bottom and up sides of prepared pan. Bake for 10 minutes. Transfer to a wire rack to cool.

② For filling: In a large bowl with electric mixer on medium speed, beat cream cheese until fluffy. Gradually beat in sugar, flour and vanilla. Stop and scrape down sides of the bowl. Add eggs 1 at a time, beating after each addition. Mix in sour cream until blended. Carefully pour filling into crust.

③ Place foil-wrapped pan into a larger, deep pan. Heat water in kettle or microwave and pour into larger pan so that it reaches about halfway up the sides of cake pan.

④ Bake for 1 hour and 10 minutes, until edges are set and the center jiggles slightly when pan is shaken. Transfer to a wire rack to cool. Loosely cover cooled cake and refrigerate until cold, for at least 4 hours. Run a knife around cake to loosen from pan. Release pan sides.

⑤ For glaze: Melt white chocolate and butter in a bowl set over a saucepan of hot water, stirring often. Remove from heat; whisk in confectioners' sugar and cream to desired consistency. Drizzle glaze over cooled cake. Cut peppermint patties in half; arrange decoratively on cake.

TIP: Cheesecake will keep, covered and refrigerated, for up to 1 week.

Chocolate Hazelnut Cheesecake

CRUST

¼ cup hazelnuts, chopped and skinned

10 ounces chocolate sandwich cookies (about 25 cookies)

4 tablespoons (½ stick) unsalted butter, melted

FILLING

3 packages (8-ounce size) cream cheese, at room temperature

1 cup granulated sugar

½ cup sour cream

1 teaspoon vanilla extract

3 large eggs

¾ cup chocolate-hazelnut spread (such as Nutella)

Cheesecake has a bad reputation for being hard to make. Truth is, this one comes together in minutes.

1. For crust: Preheat oven to 350°F. Wrap foil around outside and up sides of a 9-inch springform pan. In a food processor, pulse hazelnuts until chopped. Add cookies; pulse into crumbs. Add melted butter; process until crumbs are moist and hold together when squeezed. Press crumbs into bottom and up sides of prepared pan. Bake for 10 minutes. Transfer to a wire rack to cool.

2. For filling: In a large bowl with electric mixer on medium speed, beat cream cheese until fluffy. Gradually beat in sugar, sour cream and vanilla. Stop and scrape down sides of the bowl. Add eggs 1 at a time, beating after each addition. Reserve about 1 cup of filling in a bowl; pour the rest into cooled crust. Stir hazelnut spread into reserved batter until blended. Drop spoonfuls of hazelnut–cream cheese mixture into filling in pan. Draw a knife back and forth across the batter, creating a marbled appearance.

3. Place foil-wrapped pan into a larger, deep pan. Heat water in kettle or microwave and pour into larger pan so that it reaches about halfway up the sides of the cake pan.

4. Bake for 1 hour and 10 minutes, until edges are set and center jiggles slightly when pan is shaken. Transfer to a wire rack to cool. Loosely cover cooled cake and refrigerate for at least 4 hours. Run a knife around cake to loosen from pan. Release pan sides.

TIP: Make this super-speedy by substituting a prepared crumb crust.

Perfect Raspberry Squares

Everyone needs a recipe like this in his or her dessert repertoire—
quick to make, crowd pleasing and practically foolproof.

MAKES 24

① Preheat oven to 350°F. Line a 9-by-13-inch pan with a large piece of foil
or parchment paper; butter the foil.

② In a large bowl with electric mixer on medium speed, combine flour,
oats, *both* sugars, baking soda, salt and nuts. With mixer on low speed,
add butter pieces. Beat for about 2 minutes, until blended.

③ Press about ⅔ of mixture evenly into the prepared pan. Bake for
20 minutes, until just golden. Remove pan from oven, spread jam evenly
over hot crust. Sprinkle remaining oat mixture evenly over jam. Bake
for 25 minutes, until jam bubbles and top is golden brown. Transfer to
a wire rack to cool.

3 cups all-purpose flour

2¼ cups quick oats

⅔ cup granulated sugar

⅔ cup light brown sugar

½ teaspoon baking soda

½ teaspoon salt

1 cup chopped walnuts

1½ cups (3 sticks) unsalted
butter, at room temperature, cut
into chunks, plus more for pan

1 jar (12 to 14 ounces) raspberry
jam or preserves

TIP: Lining the pan with foil makes removal of the squares for cutting very
easy—just lift out the entire block and place it on a cutting board to cut.
Use the butter clinging to the butter wrappers to grease the foil.

Cranberry Caramel Tart

SERVES 8 TO 10

CRUST

8 ounces animal crackers or shortbread cookies

1 tablespoon granulated sugar

6 tablespoons (¾ stick) unsalted butter, melted

FILLING

1 cup granulated sugar

1¼ cups heavy cream

1¾ cups fresh or frozen thawed cranberries

1½ pounds walnuts, toasted and coarsely chopped (about 5 cups)

This beautiful tart looks like it belongs in a pastry-shop window.

1. For crust: Preheat oven to 350°F. In a food processor, pulse cookies with sugar into fine crumbs. Add melted butter; process until crumbs are moist and hold together when squeezed. Press crumbs in bottom and up sides of a 9-inch pie tin, preferably one with fluted edges and a removable bottom.

2. For filling: Spread out sugar in a medium heavy skillet set over low heat. Cook for about 8 minutes, until sugar melts into golden caramel. Gently stir caramel as it cooks if spots seem to be overcooking.

3. Meanwhile, warm cream in a microwave or small saucepan over low heat. Carefully whisk warm cream into caramel; mixture will bubble vigorously. Cook, still over low heat, until all the caramel pieces melt, for about 8 minutes, stirring often. Pour caramel into a medium bowl; cool for 5 minutes.

4. Fold cranberries and walnuts into caramel until coated. Scrape mixture into prepared crust. Bake for 40 minutes, until cranberries are soft and caramel bubbles. Transfer to a wire rack to cool. Run a knife around pie edges to loosen from pan. Carefully remove pan sides.

TIP: Be patient when making the caramel. The sugar needs to melt over low heat so as not to get scorched.

Glazed White Fruitcake

CAKE

1 cup golden raisins, chopped

¾ cup dried or candied pineapple chunks, chopped

¾ cup dried or candied mango or papaya chunks, chopped

¾ cup dried sweetened cherries, chopped

¾ cup coconut flakes (sweetened or unsweetened)

¼ cup fresh lemon juice plus ¼ cup water

1 cup (2 sticks) unsalted butter, at room temperature, plus more for pan

2 cups confectioners' sugar

4 large eggs, separated

1 teaspoon vanilla extract

½ teaspoon lemon extract

1½ cups all-purpose flour

1 cup pecans, chopped

GLAZE

1 cup confectioners' sugar

2 tablespoons heavy cream or half-and-half

This update on traditional fruitcake gives the option of using dried fruit rather than candied. Hence, you can take advantage of all the organic dried fruits now available.

1. For cake: In a large bowl, combine raisins, pineapple, mango, cherries and coconut. Add juice and water; refrigerate fruits overnight.

2. Preheat oven to 275°F. Line a 9-by-5-inch loaf pan with parchment paper; lightly butter and flour paper.

3. In a large bowl with electric mixer on high speed, beat butter and sugar until blended. Beat in egg yolks and *both* extracts. Mix in flour. Scrape dough into a large bowl. Gently fold in dried fruit (with its juice) and nuts. Wash and dry mixing bowl.

4. In a large bowl with electric mixer on high speed, beat egg whites until soft peaks form. Fold whites into cake batter until blended. Scoop batter into the prepared pan. Bake for about 1½ hours, until firm and golden. Transfer to a wire rack to cool. Invert cake onto rack and cool completely.

5. For glaze: In a small bowl, whisk confectioners' sugar and cream until a glaze forms. Using whisk, drizzle glaze over cooled fruitcake.

TIP: Feel free to substitute any dried fruit, in any amounts, that you like. Just aim for about 4 cups dried fruit and 1 cup nuts.

Peanut Butter Balls

For those of us who believe that the popular candy bar doesn't contain enough peanut filling, these delicious confections are the perfect treat. Even better—they are super-easy to make and will keep for months in the freezer.

MAKES 50

1. In a large bowl with electric mixer on high speed, beat peanut butter, butter, salt and vanilla until blended. Add sugar and cracker crumbs; beat until blended. Dough should hold together when squeezed.

2. Roll dough between your palms into 1-inch balls. Place balls on a parchment-lined baking sheet or platter. Transfer sheet to refrigerator; chill candy for 1 hour, until firm.

3. Melt chocolate and shortening in microwave, double boiler or using a metal bowl placed over a pot of simmering water. Dip each candy in melted chocolate, covering completely. Remove ball from melted chocolate, allowing excess chocolate to drip back into bowl. Return candies to lined sheet; refrigerate until set.

2 cups creamy peanut butter

4 tablespoons (½ stick) unsalted butter, at room temperature

¼ teaspoon salt

½ teaspoon vanilla extract

2½ to 2¾ cups confectioners' sugar

½ cup finely crushed animal crackers or vanilla wafers

1 package (12 ounces) semisweet chocolate chips

2 tablespoons shortening

TIP: To quickly crush crackers for the filling, seal them in a resealable bag and pound on the bag with a rolling pin.

Red Velvet Bouquet Cake

SERVES 12

CAKE

2½ cups cake flour (not self-rising)

¼ cup unsweetened cocoa

1½ teaspoons baking powder

12 tablespoons (1½ sticks) unsalted butter, at room temperature, plus more for pans

2 cups granulated sugar

3 large eggs

1 teaspoon vanilla extract

¼ teaspoon salt

2 bottles (1-ounce size) liquid red food coloring

3 tablespoons brewed coffee

1 cup buttermilk

1 tablespoon white vinegar

1 teaspoon baking soda

FROSTING

1 box (8 ounces) cream cheese, at room temperature

½ cup (1 stick) unsalted butter, at room temperature

1 teaspoon vanilla extract

4 cups sifted confectioners' sugar

Topping a luscious red velvet cake with a bouquet of holiday poinsettias makes for a stunning presentation. Bake in 3 6-inch pans for a small, tall cake or 2 9-inch pans for a more traditionally sized cake.

1. For cake: Preheat oven to 350°F. Lightly butter 3 6-inch round cake pans or 2 9-inch round cake pans. Line with parchment paper; butter and flour pans.

2. In a medium bowl, sift together flour, cocoa and baking powder. In a large bowl with electric mixer on high speed, beat butter and sugar until light and fluffy. Add eggs, 1 at a time, beating well after each addition. Add vanilla, salt, food coloring and coffee; beat until combined. Reduce speed to low; alternately add dry ingredients and buttermilk. Beat until just combined.

3. In a small bowl, combine vinegar and baking soda. Add to batter; beat just until blended. Pour batter into prepared pans. Bake until toothpick inserted in the center comes out clean; 25 minutes for small pans, 30 minutes for large pans. Transfer to a wire rack; cool for 15 minutes. Run a knife around edges of cake; turn cakes out onto rack and cool completely.

4. For frosting: In a large bowl with electric mixer on high speed, beat cream cheese and butter until fluffy. Beat in vanilla. Gradually add confectioners' sugar, beating until fluffy.

5. Frost cakes as desired. Transfer to refrigerator to set.

6. Using a serrated knife, carve a block of flower foam into a dome shape that roughly fits the top of the cake. Cover entire dome in plastic wrap, taping the bottom so the wrap stays in place. Clip poinsettia blossoms leaving 2-inch stems. Carefully poke stems into foam block. Pack flowers tightly to entirely cover block. Place block on top of cake. Serve immediately.

TIP: Touching a poinsettia leaf may cause irritation; remember to wrap the foam block and remove the flower "top" before cutting the cake. You don't want the plant to touch the cake.

Great Pumpkin Cake with Cinnamon Glaze

SERVES 16

CAKE

4 cups cake flour (not self-rising)

4 teaspoons baking powder

1 teaspoon baking soda

1 teaspoon salt

1 tablespoon ground ginger

1 tablespoon ground cinnamon

1 teaspoon ground nutmeg

½ teaspoon ground cloves

1 cup (2 sticks) unsalted butter, room temperature, plus more for pan

2½ cups granulated sugar

4 large eggs

1 cup buttermilk

1 can (15 ounces) pumpkin puree (not pumpkin pie mix)

1 tablespoon vanilla extract

GLAZE

1 cup confectioners' sugar

½ teaspoon ground cinnamon

2 to 4 tablespoons heavy cream or half-and-half

This moist and spicy cake makes a beautiful not-too-sweet dessert or a delicious breakfast treat.

1. Preheat oven to 350°F. Generously butter a 12- to 14-cup Bundt pan. Dust with flour; tap out excess.

2. For cake: In a medium bowl, whisk flour, baking powder, baking soda, salt, ginger, cinnamon, nutmeg and cloves.

3. In a large bowl with electric mixer on high speed, beat butter and sugar until fluffy. Add eggs, 1 at a time, beating well after each addition and scraping down sides of bowl as needed. Reduce speed to low. Alternately add dry ingredients and buttermilk, beating until just combined. Add pumpkin and vanilla; beat until combined. Pour batter into prepared pan.

4. Bake cake for 1 hour, until firm and a toothpick inserted in the center comes out with a few moist crumbs. Transfer to a wire rack; let cool for 30 minutes. Carefully turn cake onto rack to cool completely.

5. For glaze: In a medium bowl, whisk together sugar and cinnamon. Whisk in cream until of desired consistency. Drizzle over cooled cake.

TIP: Recipe makes a big cake—be sure to use a large-size Bundt pan.

French Almond Cake

This simply elegant cake gets its super-moist texture and intense almond flavor from almond paste. Find it in the baking section of your supermarket.

SERVES 8

1. Preheat oven to 350°F. Butter bottom and sides of an 8-inch round cake pan. Line bottom of the pan with parchment paper; butter the paper.

2. In large bowl with electric mixer on medium speed, beat almond paste and sugar until small crumbs form. Add butter; beat 5 minutes, until light and fluffy. Stop and scrape sides of bowl as needed. Blend in honey. Add eggs 1 at a time, beating well after each addition. Add amaretto, flour and a pinch of salt; beat until just combined.

3. Spread batter into prepared pan; smooth the top. Bake for about 28 minutes, or until cake is golden and top springs back when touched. Transfer to a wire rack to cool. Run a spatula around edges of cake to release from pan. Let cool completely. Dust with confectioners' sugar; arrange raspberries in center of cake.

TIP: Don't overbake or the cake will be dry. Although the baked top will be golden, the center of the cake should not be firm to the touch.

1 tube (7 ounces) almond paste

¼ cup granulated sugar

½ cup (1 stick) cold unsalted butter, diced, plus more for pan

2 tablespoons honey

3 large eggs

1 tablespoon amaretto liqueur or ½ teaspoon almond extract

½ cup all-purpose flour

Salt

Confectioners' sugar and fresh raspberries, for garnish

Brown Sugar Toasted Pecan Pie

No holiday dessert table is complete without a pecan pie.

1. For pie: Preheat oven to 350°F. Place oven rack in bottom third of oven. On a lightly floured surface, carefully roll pie crust. Press dough into a shallow pie tin or tart pan with removable bottom.

2. In a medium saucepan over medium-low heat, combine the yolks, brown sugar, corn syrup, cream, butter and salt. Heat just until the edges simmer; do not boil. Cook for about 6 minutes, stirring constantly, until thickened and a candy thermometer registers 160°F. Pour mixture through a strainer set over a mixing bowl. Stir in vanilla.

3. Evenly spread nuts over the chilled pastry crust, top sides up. Pour filling evenly over nuts. Bake for 30 minutes, until filling is puffed, golden and just set. Transfer to a wire rack to cool.

4. For whipped cream: In a large bowl with electric mixer on high speed, whip cream and syrup until soft peaks form. Serve immediately.

TIP: To toast pecans, place on a baking sheet and bake for about 8 minutes in a 350°F oven until lightly browned and fragrant.

SERVES 8 TO 10

PIE

1 refrigerated pie crust, thawed

4 egg yolks

½ cup dark brown sugar

⅓ cup dark corn syrup

¼ cup heavy cream

4 tablespoons (½ stick) unsalted butter

¼ teaspoon salt

1 tablespoon vanilla extract

1½ cups pecan halves, toasted

WHIPPED CREAM

1 cup heavy cream

1½ tablespoons pure maple syrup

Gifts to Give

Ideas for quick-to-make presents for the home.

Do-It-Yourself Spice Packets

For friends who like to bake, surprise them with small jars of baking spice blends. Package in small glass jars, or, even better, old-fashioned spice jars with glass or cork tops.

Makes about 5 tablespoons each

PUMPKIN PIE SPICE

3 tablespoons ground cinnamon

1 tablespoon ground ginger

1 teaspoon ground cloves

½ teaspoon ground nutmeg

¼ teaspoon ground cardamom

APPLE PIE SPICE

2 tablespoons ground cinnamon

2 teaspoons ground allspice

1 teaspoon ground nutmeg

1 teaspoon ground ginger

¼ teaspoon ground cardamom

In a small bowl, combine all ingredients for desired mix; stir to blend well. Store in a small, airtight container.

Pinecone Fire Starters

Sweetly scented pinecone fire starters make an excellent wintertime hostess gift.

Makes 2

SUPPLIES

2 large fat pinecones

Ball of twine or candle wick

2 heatproof small, narrow bowls/containers for setting the pinecones in wax

Unflavored cooking oil (such as canola, sunflower or safflower)

Medium saucepan and medium (at least 2-cup) glass measuring cup with a spout

Candle wax beads or beeswax (about ¾ cup per pinecone)

Essential oil of your choice (such as cinnamon or clove)

1. Wrap twine around and through points at the base of each pinecone. Wrap twine at least 10 times around cone, keeping along the bottom half of the cone. Leave a long tail of twine hanging out.

2. Heavily coat the inside of each bowl with oil (this helps the pinecone to release from the bowl after wax hardens.) Place a wrapped pinecone in each bowl, letting the end of the twine trail outside the bowl.

3. Bring water to boil in saucepot. Carefully set a glass measuring cup in the boiling water. The water should come about halfway up the sides of the measuring cup. Pour in about 1 cup of wax beads and a few drops of essential oil. Melt wax, checking pot frequently to assure water hasn't evaporated. When wax is melted, carefully lift cup out of water (cup will be hot) and slowly pour the hot wax into the bowls with the pinecones. Wax should come about 1 inch up the sides of the cone. Let wax set about 20 minutes. (Setting time will depend on size of container.) Run a knife around the edges of the bowl to loosen wax. Carefully grasp pinecone and twist out of bowl. Cut the wick. Let sit overnight in a cool place to firmly set the wax.

Homemade Holiday Pincushion

This charming pincushion is easy to make and a great way to use up scraps of fabric. If you can't find a wooden bowl, substitute a vintage china teacup.

Makes 1

SUPPLIES

Small wooden bowl

Scrap of fabric, about 3 inches wider than the bowl

Fiberfill baking

Hot glue gun

Glass head straight pins

1. Cut a circle of fabric 3 inches wider than the bowl. Hand-sew a running stitch around circle, stitching about ½ inch from the edge. Before cutting your thread and removing the needle, pull the thread tight to gather your fabric into a pouch. Stuff the pouch with fiberfill until very full. Pull on the thread to close the opening. Stitch the opening closed.

2. Drizzle hot glue over the bottom and sides of the bowl. Place fabric ball in cup, stitched-side down. Press down to affix to the bowl. Let dry. Add pins.

Bubbling Bath Cubes

Handmade gifts come from the heart. These spa treatments make excellent gifts for teachers, tutors and grandmothers. When these sweetly scented cubes are added to a warm bath, they sizzle and bubble. They make an especially nice gift when packaged in an old-fashioned apothecary jar.

Makes 1 dozen (2 per bath)

1 cup baking soda

¾ cup cornstarch

½ cup citric acid

¼ cup granulated sugar

1 tablespoon plus 2 teaspoons almond or olive oil

10 drops essential oil, scent of choice

About 6 drops liquid food coloring, color of choice

2 teaspoons water

2 silicone ice cube trays

1. Combine baking soda, cornstarch, citric acid and sugar in food processor; pulse to combine.

2. With the processor running, drizzle almond oil and essential oil through the feed tube; process to blend. Add food coloring; pulse to blend. With the motor running, add just enough water to bring the mix to a crumbly mass. The consistency should be like damp sand. Mixture should hold its shape when squeezed.

3. Transfer mixture into ice cube trays; pressing mixture firmly into each mold. Set cubes in a cool, dry place and let dry for 2 hours or overnight. Carefully remove cubes from the tray. Cubes should feel dry and hard.

4. Package cubes into glass jars. Write scent name on a gift tag and attach to jar with a ribbon.

NOTE: Citric acid, a common food additive, is available at craft supply stores and online. The combination of citric acid and baking soda causes a bubbling chemical reaction when immersed in water.

Do-It-Yourself Drink Mixes

Got a friend who loves coffee shop specialty drinks? Give her the ability to make these treats in her own kitchen.

INSTANT CAPPUCCINO MIX

Makes about 2¼ cups

1 cup powdered chocolate milk mix
¾ cup powdered non-dairy creamer
½ cup instant coffee
½ teaspoon ground cinnamon
½ teaspoon ground nutmeg

In a medium bowl, combine all ingredients. Store in an airtight container. To serve: Place 1 heaping tablespoon mix in a cup or mug. Add 1 cup boiling water and stir.

＊ ＊ ＊

MOCHA COFFEE MIX IN A JAR

Makes about 3½ cups

1 cup nonfat dry milk powder
1¼ cups granulated sugar
⅔ cup powdered non-dairy creamer
½ cup unsweetened cocoa
½ cup instant coffee
1 teaspoon ground cinnamon

Combine all ingredients in a food processor; pulse until ground and blended. To serve:

Place rounded ¼ cup mixture in a cup or mug. Add ¾ cup boiling water and stir until mix is dissolved.

＊ ＊ ＊

HOMEMADE CHAI TEA MIX

Makes about 2 cups

¾ cup and 2 tablespoons brown sugar
1 teaspoon vanilla extract
⅓ cup nonfat dry milk powder
⅓ cup powdered non-dairy creamer
¾ teaspoon ground ginger
¾ teaspoon ground cinnamon
¼ teaspoon ground cloves
¼ teaspoon ground cardamom
Pinch black pepper

In a food processor, pulse sugar and vanilla until vanilla is incorporated. Add milk powder and non-dairy creamer; pulse to combine. Add ginger, cinnamon, cloves, cardamom and pepper; process until mixture is the consistency of fine powder. To serve: Stir 2 heaping tablespoons mixture into a mug of hot tea.

Christmas Gifts

As you already know, I *love* Christmas. I love everything about it. I make the most of a season that often seems too short. Within the space of a few weeks, I host two Christmas Teas, as well as Christmas Open Houses at home and at the office. Plus, like all of us, I do the shopping, wrapping, cooking. . . . That's all part of the Christmas experience. It's exhausting and yet energizing. But I enjoy this time of year so much, I try to share that enjoyment every way I can.

I believe that the best gifts I can give my friends and family are those that come directly from my own hands and from my heart. This usually means something I've knit, cooked or baked. With a homemade gift, I'm giving a piece of me—of my time and skill. (Needless to say, it's also the kind of gift I prefer to receive.)

One of the best examples I have of this type of gift, one that comes from the heart, is what my sons Ted and Dale gave my parents.

Like me, both my parents loved Christmas. My father used to put up multiple strands of outdoor lights and Mom painstakingly decorated the house. As they grew older this became difficult and then, eventually, impossible. One Christmas when Ted and Dale were in college, they had a hard time figuring out what to get for their grandparents, since as students they had no money. They came to me with an idea. They would decorate their grandparents' house in Yakima—some distance away—and then in January return to take everything down. It was a perfect gift, the best they could have given my parents. I doubt there was anyone in Yakima who didn't hear about these wonderful grandsons. The time they spent with my parents meant far more to Mom and Dad than anything they could have purchased.

When our children were still living at home, I wanted them to realize how blessed our family was and that there were children in our town who wouldn't have a gift under the Christmas tree—children who might not have a tree at all. So I took them to a charity tree, where they each chose the name of a child close to their own ages. I gave them money to shop for that child. They understood this would mean one less gift for them but not once did I hear a word of complaint. They each purchased a gift for "their" child, wrapped it themselves and sometimes included a handwritten letter wishing the recipient a Merry Christmas. Then we brought the gift back to the Giving Tree.

I practice the same principle with my grandchildren now, but I do it on their birthdays. My grandkids don't need another toy that will all too soon be forgotten. Instead I let them choose a gift from the World Vision catalogue to be sent to another child, usually in another country. My grandson Isaiah chose chickens for a Third World village the year he turned six, and his cousin James wanted a goat and soccer balls for the children in an African village. He likes playing soccer and felt other children would, too. Jazmine, my oldest granddaughter, decided to pay for the education of a young girl in Thailand for a year. I've been deeply impressed by how thoughtful and caring they are.

Growing up, I learned that Christmas is a time of giving to others. My parents, Ted and Connie Adler, were two of the most generous people I've ever known. Every Christmas, my mother and I baked cookies and made hand-dipped chocolates, which Mom arranged in baskets and distributed to others. There was always a basket for our parish priest and one for the nuns in our local convent. She remembered the neighbors, the mail carrier, the milkman and my father's business associates. She didn't forget family, either. My aunts and uncles received Mom's Christmas baskets every year, too.

In the Christmas prologue to my story "5-B Poppy Lane" (which appears in *Christmas in Cedar Cove*), Charlotte Rhodes brings Helen a jar of homemade green tomato mincemeat. I chose that because my friend Laura Early brings me a jar or two every year, since she knows how much I enjoy it. (Don't tell Laura but I've been known to eat it straight from the jar!)

Whatever gifts you choose to make for those you love, I hope you'll take a look at the following recipes and be inspired.

Triple Ginger Chocolate Chunk Cookies

MAKES 24

1½ cups all-purpose flour

2 tablespoons unsweetened cocoa

1½ teaspoons ground ginger

1 teaspoon ground cinnamon

¼ teaspoon ground cloves

¼ teaspoon ground nutmeg

½ cup (1 stick) unsalted butter, at room temperature

½ cup brown sugar

1 teaspoon minced, peeled fresh ginger

⅓ cup molasses

1 teaspoon baking soda

6 ounces best-quality semisweet chocolate, cut into small chunks, or chips

¼ cup chopped crystallized ginger

Granulated sugar for coating

The classic chocolate chip cookie takes a holiday turn by partnering with a triple shot of sharp ginger.

1 In a medium bowl, combine flour, cocoa, ground ginger, cinnamon, cloves and nutmeg.

2 In a large bowl with electric mixer on high speed, beat butter, brown sugar and fresh ginger until blended. Add molasses; beat until combined.

3 In a small bowl, dissolve baking soda in 2 teaspoons very hot water; add to batter. Add flour mixture and beat until just combined. Fold in chocolate chunks and crystallized ginger. Refrigerate for at least 1 hour, or overnight.

4 Preheat oven to 350°F. Line 2 baking sheets with parchment paper. Roll dough between your palms into a walnut-size ball. Roll balls in granulated sugar to coat; place on prepared sheets about 2 inches apart. Bake for 10 minutes, until the surfaces crack, cookies are firm around edges but still slightly soft in center. Let cool on pan for 5 minutes; transfer to a wire rack to cool completely.

TIP: Chocolate chips work fine here, but uneven chunks pump the flavor up a notch.

Shown on page 139.

Almond Joy to the World

The first few candies you dip may be a bit messy—but you will quickly get the hang of the coating technique. Don't worry; the messy candies taste just as good as the perfect ones!

MAKES 50

1. Line a large rimmed baking sheet with foil or parchment paper; coat with nonstick cooking spray.

2. In a large bowl, combine condensed milk, *both* extracts and salt. Gradually fold in sugar until a thick dough forms. Fold in coconut until blended.

3. Roll dough between your palms to make 1-inch balls; place on prepared sheet. Lightly press an almond into each candy. Place sheet in refrigerator; chill candy for 1 hour, until firm.

4. Melt chocolate chips and shortening in either a microwave, with a double boiler or by using a metal bowl placed over a pot of simmering water. Let mixture cool slightly. Dip each candy in melted chocolate, covering completely. Return candies to lined sheet. Refrigerate until chocolate sets.

1 can (7 ounces) sweetened condensed milk

½ teaspoon vanilla extract

½ teaspoon coconut extract

Pinch salt

2½ cups confectioners' sugar

1 bag (14 ounces) sweetened coconut flakes

50 whole almonds, roasted or raw

1 pound semisweet chocolate chips

1 tablespoon shortening

TIP: Like all chocolate candies, these store best chilled in the refrigerator or freezer.

Cappuccino Snickerdoodles with Mocha Glaze

MAKES 46

COOKIES

2½ cups all-purpose flour

5 teaspoons ground cinnamon

2 teaspoons baking soda

2 teaspoons cream of tartar

1 teaspoon ground nutmeg

½ teaspoon salt

½ cup (1 stick) unsalted butter, at room temperature

½ cup shortening

1 cup granulated sugar, plus more for coating

½ cup brown sugar

1 large egg

1 tablespoon instant espresso powder dissolved in 1 tablespoon hot coffee or water

1 teaspoon vanilla extract

GLAZE

1 cup confectioners' sugar

1 tablespoon unsweetened cocoa

1 tablespoon espresso powder, dissolved in 1 tablespoon hot coffee or water

4 tablespoons heavy cream, or as needed

Although a cookie inspired by a coffee drink seems like a grown-up taste, the sweet, spicy flavor of these chewy gems will appeal to all mocha lovers.

1. Preheat oven to 350°F. Line 2 baking sheets with parchment paper.

2. For cookies: In a medium bowl, combine flour, cinnamon, baking soda, cream of tartar, nutmeg and salt. In a large bowl with electric mixer on high speed, beat butter, shortening and *both* sugars until light and fluffy. Add egg, dissolved espresso powder and vanilla; beat until combined. Gradually add the dry ingredients until just blended.

3. Roll dough between your palms to make 1-inch balls. Roll balls in granulated sugar to coat; place on prepared sheets about 2 inches apart. Bake for 10 minutes, until tops are cracked and just set. Let cool on pan for 5 minutes; transfer to wire racks to cool completely.

4. For glaze: In a small bowl, whisk confectioners' sugar and cocoa. In another bowl, combine dissolved espresso powder and cream. Whisk sugar mixture and coffee cream until a smooth glaze forms. Drizzle over cooled cookies.

TIP: Instant espresso powder is not the same as instant coffee. It's often found in the Spanish food aisle. You may substitute instant coffee, but the flavor won't be as strong.

Chocolate-Toffee Chewies

MAKES 24

½ cup all-purpose flour

1 teaspoon baking powder

¼ teaspoon salt

1 pound semisweet chocolate, chopped

4 tablespoons (½ stick) unsalted butter

1¾ cups brown sugar

4 large eggs

1 tablespoon vanilla extract

5 chocolate-covered English toffee bars (1.4-ounce size), such as Heath, coarsely chopped

1 cup toasted, chopped pecans

Be warned, this is an extremely addictive cookie—intense chocolate encases sweet bites of toffee and mellow pecans.

1. In a small bowl, combine flour, baking powder and salt. Melt chopped chocolate and butter in either a microwave, with a double boiler or by using a metal bowl placed over a pot of simmering water.

2. In a large bowl with electric mixer on high speed, beat sugar and eggs for 5 minutes, until thick. Pour in chocolate mixture and vanilla; beat until blended. Stir in flour mixture, then candy and pecans. Refrigerate dough for at least 45 minutes or up to overnight.

3. Preheat oven to 350°F. Line 2 baking sheets with parchment paper. Drop batter by ¼ cupfuls onto prepared sheets, spacing 2 inches apart. Bake for 14 minutes, until tops are shiny, dry and cracked, yet cookies are soft to the touch. Cool on sheets for 5 minutes. Transfer to wire racks to cool completely.

TIP: For the chewiest texture, don't overbake. Cookies should still be soft and gooey in the center.

Peppermint Patty Thins

A delicious cross between crisp chocolate cookie and creamy peppermint, this treat makes a great addition to a gift basket.

1. In a large bowl with electric mixer on low speed, cream the sugar, butter, *both* extracts and half-and-half. Increase speed to medium; beat 2 minutes until completely blended and pasty.

2. Line a large baking sheet with foil or parchment paper. Scoop up 1 tablespoon of dough; roll dough between your palms. Place a ball on the flat side of a wafer; press down with your fingers to completely cover one side of the cookie. Arrange cookies on prepared sheet; refrigerate for 30 minutes, until firm.

3. Melt chocolate and shortening until completely smooth, in either a microwave, with a double boiler or by using a metal bowl placed over a pot of simmering water. Let mixture cool slightly. Dip each covered cookie in melted chocolate, covering completely. Let excess chocolate drip back into bowl. Return cookies to lined sheet. Refrigerate for 30 minutes or until the chocolate sets.

TIP: Peppermint extracts vary in strength; taste test yours as you add it to the dough.

2 cups plus 2 tablespoons confectioners' sugar

2 tablespoons unsalted butter, softened

1 teaspoon peppermint extract

½ teaspoon vanilla extract

2 tablespoons half-and-half or heavy cream

24 thin chocolate wafer cookies, such as Nabisco Famous

1 cup semi- or bittersweet chocolate chips

1 tablespoon shortening

Pecan Turtle Brownies

MAKES 20

CARAMEL

¼ cup plus 2 tablespoons heavy cream

¼ teaspoon salt

¼ cup water

2 tablespoons corn syrup

1¼ cup granulated sugar

2 tablespoons unsalted butter

½ teaspoon vanilla extract

BROWNIES

½ cup (1 stick) unsalted butter, cut into pieces, plus more for pan

4 ounces semisweet chocolate chips

2 ounces unsweetened chocolate, chopped

¾ cup all-purpose flour

½ teaspoon baking powder

¼ teaspoon salt

2 large eggs

1 cup granulated sugar

2 teaspoons vanilla extract

20 pecan halves, toasted

Two perfect treats, brownies and turtle candies, come together in this special bar. Note: You'll need a candy thermometer to assure perfect caramel consistency.

1. For caramel: Pour cream into a glass measuring cup; stir in salt to dissolve. In a small heavy saucepan over medium-high heat, combine water and corn syrup. Gently stir sugar into pot. Cover and bring to a boil. Cook for 4 minutes, until sugar is completely dissolved, without stirring. Uncover and cook for 4 minutes, without stirring. Reduce heat to medium-low. Cook for 2 more minutes, until golden and a candy thermometer registers about 360°F.

2. Remove pot from heat and carefully pour cream into center of pot. Mixture will bubble vigorously; stir until cream is incorporated. Once bubbling eases, stir in butter and vanilla. Lightly coat a glass measuring cup with butter; pour caramel into prepared cup.

3. For brownies: Preheat oven to 325°F. Set oven rack to lower-middle position. Line a 9-inch square baking pan with foil or parchment paper, letting foil hang over sides of pan. Lightly butter bottom and sides of foil.

4. In a medium heatproof bowl, combine butter, semisweet and unsweetened chocolates. Microwave until melted, stirring at least once; set aside to cool.

5. In a small bowl, whisk flour, baking powder and salt. In a large bowl, whisk eggs, sugar and vanilla until blended. Whisk cooled chocolate mixture into egg mixture. Fold in flour mixture until blended. Pour batter into prepared pan. Drizzle about ¼ of the caramel over top. Using tip of a knife, swirl caramel and batter. Bake for 35 minutes, until a toothpick inserted into center comes out with a few moist crumbs. Transfer to a wire rack to cool.

6. Warm remaining caramel (you should have about ¾ cup) in microwave until pourable but still thick (do not boil), stirring once. Pour caramel over brownies; evenly spread caramel. Refrigerate brownies, uncovered, for at least 2 hours.

7. Using foil extensions, lift cold brownies from pan. Run a knife around edges of brownies to loosen sides from foil (caramel may stick). Peel

away foil. Using a sharp knife, cut brownies into squares. Press a pecan half onto middle of each brownie.

TIP: Pour the finished caramel directly into a glass measuring cup that has been sprayed with nonstick spray or coated with butter. This makes for safe reheating in the microwave, foolproof pouring and easy clean-up.

Glazed Cranberry White Chocolate Bars

These fancy double-glazed bars only *look* hard to make. They are sturdy enough to pack and ship.

MAKES 24

1. Preheat oven to 350°F. Lightly butter a 9-by-13-inch baking pan.

2. For base: In a large bowl with electric mixer on high speed, beat butter and sugar until fluffy. Add vanilla and eggs, one at a time, beating well after each addition. Stir in flour, baking powder, ginger, nutmeg and salt until combined. Stir in white chocolate and cranberries. Spread batter in prepared pan. Bake for 25 minutes, until light golden yet still slightly soft in the center. Transfer to a wire rack to cool.

3. For frosting: In a large bowl with electric mixer on medium speed, beat cream cheese, lemon juice and vanilla until blended. Gradually beat in the confectioners' sugar until blended and of spreading consistency. Spread the frosting evenly over cooled cake. Immediately scatter chopped cranberries on top of the frosting.

4. For drizzle: In a microwave or double boiler, melt white chocolate until smooth and of drizzling consistency. Drizzle over frosted bars.

TIP: Keep an eye on the bars at the end of their baking time, making sure not to overbake them. The center should still be soft.

BASE

1 cup (2 sticks) unsalted butter, at room temperature, plus more for pan

1¼ cups brown sugar, firmly packed

1 teaspoon vanilla extract

3 large eggs

1½ cups all-purpose flour

½ teaspoon baking powder

½ teaspoon ground ginger

½ teaspoon ground nutmeg

½ teaspoon salt

1 cup white chocolate chips

½ cup dried cranberries

FROSTING

4 ounces cream cheese, at room temperature

2 tablespoons fresh lemon juice

½ teaspoon vanilla extract

2 cups confectioners' sugar

½ cup dried cranberries, chopped

DRIZZLE

½ cup white chocolate chips

Linzer Cookies

COOKIES

1 cup blanched or sliced almonds

¾ cup granulated sugar

2¼ cups all-purpose flour

½ teaspoon ground cinnamon

¼ teaspoon ground cloves

¼ teaspoon salt

1 cup (2 sticks) unsalted butter, at room temperature

1 teaspoon vanilla extract

2 large egg yolks

1 teaspoon grated lemon zest

Confectioners' sugar, for garnish

FILLING

½ cup semi- or bittersweet chocolate, chips or chopped

½ cup seedless raspberry jam

Mini Linzer tortes made extra special with an added layer of dark chocolate.

1. For cookies: Preheat oven to 350°F. Place almonds on a baking sheet and toast for about 8 minutes, or until lightly browned, stirring often. Transfer to a food processor; add ¼ cup of the sugar and pulse until finely ground.

2. In a medium bowl, combine flour, cinnamon, cloves and salt. In a large bowl with electric mixer on high speed, beat butter and remaining ½ cup sugar until light and fluffy. Beat in the vanilla, yolks and zest. Beat in the ground almonds and flour mixture, beating until just blended. Form the dough into 2 disks; wrap tightly in plastic. Refrigerate until firm, for at least 1 hour or up to 3 days.

3. Preheat oven to 350°F. Line 2 baking sheets with parchment paper. On a lightly floured surface, roll out 1 disk of dough to about ¼-inch thick. Using a 2-inch-round cookie cutter, cut out as many cookies as possible. Place cookies about 1 inch apart on prepared sheet. Use a smaller (about 1 inch) cookie cutter to cut out the centers of half of the cookies on the baking sheet. Reroll any scraps; cut out cookies in the same manner. You should have about 26 cookies with cutouts in the middle and 26 uncut cookies. Repeat with remaining disk of dough.

4. Bake cookies for 12 minutes, until lightly browned. Transfer to a wire rack to cool.

5. For filling: Melt chocolate chips in microwave. Spread a small amount of chocolate on top of the cooled uncut cookies (the bottom half of the cookie sandwich). Place in refrigerator for 30 minutes for chocolate to set. Meanwhile, sprinkle cutout cookies with confectioners' sugar. Remove chocolate-coated cookies from refrigerator. Spread a thin layer of jam on top of the chocolate layer. Top with cutout cookie.

TIP: You can make the dough up to 3 days in advance. Store, tightly covered, in the refrigerator.

Coffee Shop Hazelnut and Dried Cherry Biscotti

MAKES 36

3¼ cups all-purpose flour

1 tablespoon baking powder

¼ teaspoon salt

1½ cups granulated sugar

10 tablespoons (1¼ sticks) unsalted butter, melted

3 large eggs

1 tablespoon vanilla extract

1 tablespoon orange zest

1¼ cups hazelnuts, toasted, skinned and coarsely chopped

1½ cups dried cherries, chopped

1 large egg white, lightly beaten, for wash

Given their sturdy texture, biscotti are a good choice for packing and shipping. They also keep well—store in an airtight container for up to 1 week.

1. Preheat oven to 350°F. Line a baking sheet with parchment paper. In a medium bowl, combine flour, baking powder and salt. In another large bowl, whisk sugar, melted butter, eggs, vanilla and orange zest. Fold in flour mixture until well blended. Stir in hazelnuts and dried cherries.

2. Turn dough out onto a lightly floured counter. Divide dough in half. Using floured hands, shape each portion into 13-by-3 inch logs. Press down slightly on logs so they are flattened on the bottom. Transfer logs to prepared baking sheet, spacing 2 inches apart. Brush top and sides of dough log with egg white wash.

3. Bake for 30 minutes, until golden brown. Transfer sheet to a wire rack; cool for 15 minutes. Maintain oven temperature.

4. Transfer logs to counter. Using a serrated knife, carefully cut logs on the diagonal into ½-inch-wide slices. Arrange slices, cut side down, on the same baking sheet. Bake for 10 minutes. Flip cookies; bake for 8 minutes, until just golden. Transfer cookies to a wire rack to cool.

TIP: Look for packages of prepeeled, chopped hazelnuts in the baking section of your supermarket.

Chocolate-Glazed Shortbread Fingers

Because of its buttery texture, shortbread keeps well—up to 1 week in a sealed container.

1. For shortbread: In a large bowl with electric mixer on high speed, beat butter until light and fluffy. Add sugar and vanilla; beat until fluffy, scraping down the sides of the bowl as needed. Reduce speed; beat in flour and salt until just blended.

2. Turn dough out onto a lightly floured surface. Using floured hands or rolling pin, pat or roll dough to a ½-inch-thick rectangle, about 6-by-9 inches. Using a sharp knife, cut into 1-by-3-inch rectangles; transfer to a parchment-paper lined baking sheet. Refrigerate until firm.

3. Preheat oven to 350°F. Bake shortbread for 20 minutes, until just golden around the edges. Transfer to a wire rack to cool.

4. For glaze: Melt chocolate and shortening in microwave or in a bowl set over a pot of hot water. Stir until completely smooth. Using a fork, drizzle warm glaze over cooled shortbread.

TIP: Remember to reduce the mixer speed before adding the flour, or it will fly everywhere!

MAKES 18

SHORTBREAD

1 cup (2 sticks) unsalted butter, at room temperature

½ cup confectioners' sugar

1 teaspoon vanilla extract

2 cups all-purpose flour

½ teaspoon salt

GLAZE

⅔ cup semi- or bittersweet chocolate chips

1 tablespoon shortening

Many Bean Soup Mix

MAKES 1 GIFT JAR

½ cup dried yellow split peas

⅓ cup dried green split peas

⅓ cup dried red lentils

¼ cup instant minced onion

⅓ cup dried green beans

½ teaspoon ground cumin

½ teaspoon garlic powder

Here's a gift that's good for everyone on your list. Who doesn't crave a cup of warm, homemade soup on a cold winter's night?

1. Layer all ingredients, in order listed, in a 1-pint glass jar. Store tightly covered at room temperature up to 2 months.

2. On gift tag write recipe for soup as follows:

Many Bean Soup

1 tablespoon olive oil

2 carrots, peeled and sliced

2 celery stalks, thinly sliced

Salt and black pepper

1 meaty ham hock

8 cups reduced-sodium chicken broth

1. Warm oil in a medium heavy saucepan or Dutch oven over medium heat. Add carrots and celery; season with salt and pepper. Cook for 5 minutes, stirring. Add ham hock, Many Bean Soup Mix and broth; bring to a boil. Reduce heat; bring to a simmer. Cover and simmer for 2 hours, until beans are tender, stirring occasionally.
2. Remove ham hock from pot; slice ham from bone. Trim excess fat from ham; cut into small pieces. Add ham to soup; cook until warmed through.

TIP: Many large supermarkets or health food stores allow you to buy beans out of bins, so you only need to purchase the amount you need.

Green Tomato Mincemeat

MAKES ABOUT 5 CUPS

3½ cups finely chopped green tomatoes

3½ cups finely chopped tart, firm green apples

Minced peel from 1 lemon

Minced peel from 1 orange

2 tablespoons fresh lemon juice

2 cups brown sugar

1½ cups raisins

¾ cup apple-cider vinegar

3 tablespoons light molasses

2 teaspoons ground cinnamon

½ teaspoon ground cloves

½ teaspoon ground allspice

½ teaspoon ground nutmeg

Salt and black pepper

4 tablespoons (½ stick) unsalted butter, chopped

Mincemeat is a great all-purpose gift. It's a wonderful pie or cookie filling, yet also works as a cracker or sandwich topping.

1. Combine all ingredients except butter in a large heavy saucepan or Dutch oven over medium-high heat. (Omit cloves if you plan to freeze mincemeat.) Bring just to a simmer; reduce heat and cook, uncovered, for 2 hours, stirring often. Lower heat if mixture sputters, add water if mixture becomes dry. Taste mincemeat and add sugar, salt or pepper as needed.

2. Once mixture reaches desired thickness, stir in butter until melted and combined. Pour into resealable container or jar.

3. To can, pour hot mixture into hot, sterile jars, leaving ½-inch headspace for expansion, and seal promptly. Process in boiling water bath for 20 minutes. Store in a cool dry place.

4. To freeze, let mixture cool; pack cold mincemeat into resealable containers, leaving 1-inch headspace for expansion. Seal and freeze promptly.

TIP: If you like, stir in a ½ cup of brandy for an added kick.

The Kids' Table

Fun desserts for the kid in all of us.

Doughnut Hole Croquembouche

Translated from French, *croquembouche* means "crunch in the mouth." Traditionally, it's a tall pyramid of cream puffs held together by sticky caramel. Here, doughnut holes stand in for the puffs. Kids will have a blast building the tower. Croquembouche will keep, covered loosely with foil and refrigerated, for 2 days.

Makes 1

SUPPLIES

12-inch Styrofoam cone (available at floral shops and craft stores)

Wax or parchment paper and clear tape

About 50 doughnut holes, any flavor

About 50 toothpicks

Assorted candy decorations such as mini red and green M&M's, Red Hots and silver dragées

Prepared caramel sauce or dulce du leche

Sweetened coconut flakes

1. Wrap cone in parchment paper until covered. If paper isn't sticking, use some of the toothpicks. (You can remove these after doughnut holes cover the cone.) Place cone on serving platter.

2. Starting at the base of the cone, affix one ring of doughnut holes around the bottom, placing as closely together as possible. Insert toothpick through each hole and into cone to attach. Leave end of toothpick sticking out.

3. Attach second ring of doughnuts above first, packing tightly and staggering so cone is completely covered. Continue attaching doughnuts, traveling up the cone. For the top layers, cut doughnuts in half and attach cut-side against cone. This creates a tapered tree. Affix a doughnut to cover top of tree. Carefully push in all toothpicks until not visible.

4. Decorate tree with candies, pushing into gaps between holes. Use caramel sauce as "glue." Decorate platter with coconut "snow." If desired, toss coconut over entire tree to resemble snow drifts.

For the Kids

Nothing could be sweeter than creating holiday fun with Santa's littlest helpers. Just remember that when you work with kids the joy is in the process—don't expect perfection, but do expect a mess!

For a great teacher or grandma gift, help youngsters make a pinecone frame. To do: Collect lots of tiny pinecones. Using a glue gun, affix cones to a 5-by-7-inch wooden picture frame. Pack cones as tightly as you can to completely cover surface. Place a photo of the child in the frame.

Spend a fun afternoon making a snowy holiday tree. Directions: Turn a large waffle cone upside down on a plate. Fit a star tip onto an icing bag filled with prepared white frosting. Pipe stars to cover cone so it looks like a pine tree covered with snow. Decorate with silver balls and tiny candies.

Festoon your staircase and doorways with kid-made ribbon garland. Gather up all the ribbons from prior Christmas gifts and cut into 6-inch lengths. Using a glue gun (help the younger kids if needed), glue together one link; continue adding links to desired length.

Don't forget our feathered friends! Children love making treats for the birds: Thread unsalted popcorn, dried fruit, cereal and whole cranberries onto dental floss or fishing wire. String up in the boughs of a pine tree in your yard. Another idea: Dip pinecones in peanut butter, then roll in bird seed and hang on a tree.

Cooking with Grandma

Wayne and I have a total of nine grandchildren, four of whom were born within fourteen months of one another. They're the cutest, most talented, most entertaining children in the universe (although I realize they have stiff competition from everyone *else's* grandchildren).

Jazmine, our oldest, started cooking with me at two years of age. I'm not exaggerating. I was getting everything ready for a holiday meal and expected her to play contentedly on the floor, banging pots and pans. However, she had other activities in mind—she wanted to cook with me. So I let her. I brought the kitchen stepstool to my work island and showed her how to crack the eggs, add ingredients and stir. She managed all of that at age two. It was, to say the least, an eye-opening experience.

From that point forward, I didn't hesitate to allow any of the grandkids to work in the kitchen with me. Now, often the first thing they'll do when they visit is search the cupboards for a cake mix or reach for a cookbook and announce, "Grandma, let's cook!"

How can I resist?

My daughters and I have a long tradition—a Christmas slumber party. My two daughters-in-law joined in when they became part of the family. We baked cookies and rolled chocolates, but this scenario turned into something else when the grandchildren began to arrive. They wanted to be included, too.

Because cookies and candies can be a bit complicated and, er . . . messy for young children, we worked out a compromise. We decided to make small gifts for teachers, friends and anyone else they wanted to remember at Christmas.

The first Friday night of December: This is when all the grandchildren, daughters and daughters-in-law gather at the house. Once everyone shows up, Wayne and our sons quietly disappear—I have yet to figure out exactly where they go. . . .

That's when we get started in the kitchen. My daughter Jenny Adele has impressive organizational skills, so we put her in charge of amassing the ingredients and supplies.

She sets up stations all around the kitchen and family room—work areas to create soups in a jar, spice packets, cookies in a jar, plus drink mixes. Everything we need is available at these stations, including measuring cups and spoons, as well as scrupulously clean jars (which she's collected from secondhand stores throughout the year). The eating space in the kitchen is reserved for decorating the gift tags. The kids color the labels, decorate them with ribbon and glue on buttons, or whatever other decoration they choose.

At the end of the evening, we assemble all the decorated jars and prepared mixes and divide up the loot, each taking home our fair share. In addition to the many gifts we've created—it's always a productive night—we've all had tremendous fun.

A few years back, our usual plans were prevented by a rare Seattle snowstorm. The grandkids were so disappointed that I had to set a date to meet with them family by family instead of doing it all at once. With a smaller number I discovered that we could bake and cook to our hearts' content.

That particular year, Bailey and Carter, my son Ted's two children, wanted to make caramel corn. I'd never attempted it but it was a favorite of my mother's, who made it for the grandkids and great-grandkids every Christmas. I suspect this was the children's way of saying how much they missed my mother, who died six years ago. I found her recipe and together we made caramel corn—and it was just as good as Mom's.

In my story *Christmas Letters*, heroine K.O. agrees to watch her identical twin nieces, Zoe and Zara, and cooks with them. This leads to some comical moments—just as it does in life. It's natural to cook with children, boys *and* girls. They enjoy their time in the kitchen, and helping out makes them feel special. As a parent, grandparent, aunt—whatever your relationship—you have the opportunity to develop the kind of closeness that can only come from working on a shared project. You might even inspire a love of cooking that will serve them well all their lives.

The point is that these Christmas memories I've formed with my grandchildren will last far longer than any present beneath the tree.

Christmas Kitchen Sink Cookies

Also called Compost Cookies, these hefty treats can include any goodies your family likes.

1. Preheat oven to 350°F. Line 2 large baking sheets with parchment paper. In a large bowl, combine oats, flour and baking soda.

2. In a large bowl with electric mixer on high speed, cream butter, peanut butter, *both* sugars, corn syrup and vanilla until light and fluffy. Add eggs, 1 at a time, beating well after each addition.

3. With mixer on low speed, gradually beat in dry ingredients until combined. Fold in mix-ins.

4. Using an ice cream scoop, drop mounds of dough onto prepared sheets, spacing at least 2 inches apart. Flatten balls slightly. Bake for 14 minutes, or until just set. Do not overbake; cookies will be golden around the edges, but still appear wet in the center. Cool on baking sheets for 3 minutes, until firm enough to remove to wire racks. Transfer to wire racks to cool completely.

TIP: Freeze the dough balls for future cookies-in-an-instant. Place balls on a baking sheet and freeze. When completely frozen, seal balls in freezer bags. Dough will keep for several months. Bake cookies straight from the freezer; they will only need an extra few minutes in the oven.

MAKES 32

3 cups old-fashioned or quick oats

1½ cups all-purpose flour

1 teaspoon baking soda

½ cup (1 stick) unsalted butter, at room temperature

1 cup creamy peanut butter

1 cup brown sugar

¾ cup granulated sugar

1 tablespoon corn syrup

2 teaspoons vanilla extract

3 large eggs

2 cups mix-ins: red and green M&M's, chocolate chips, small pretzel pieces, butterscotch chips, corn chips, small cereal pieces

Brownie Puddle Pudding

SERVES 8

¾ cup unsweetened cocoa

½ cup all-purpose flour

4 large eggs

2 cups granulated sugar

Seeds of 1 vanilla bean or
2 teaspoons vanilla extract

1 cup (2 sticks) unsalted butter,
melted and cooled slightly, plus
more for pan

Delight youngsters by spooning this creamy pudding into teacups for serving. Top it off with a dollop of whipped cream. You can make the pudding up to 2 days in advance. Store, tightly covered, in the refrigerator.

1 Preheat oven to 325°F. Lightly butter a 2-quart casserole. In a medium bowl, sift together cocoa and flour.

2 In a large bowl with electric mixer on high speed, beat eggs, sugar and vanilla until light and fluffy. Reduce speed to low, add dry ingredients and beat until just blended. Add melted butter; beat until combined.

3 Pour batter into prepared dish. Place dish in a large roasting pan; add hot water to roasting pan so that it comes about halfway up the sides of the casserole. Bake for 55 minutes, until a toothpick inserted at the edge of the pan comes out clean, but much of the pudding looks underbaked. Transfer to a wire rack to cool.

4 Spoon cool pudding into individual teacups. Top with whipped cream. Serve cool or cold.

TIP: Extract the seeds of a vanilla bean by slicing it open lengthwise and scraping out the flavorful seeds with the back of a small spoon.

Brown Sugar Hand-Pies

Put the kids in charge of dropping the fillings into these mini pies.

1. Line a baking sheet with parchment paper. Remove pie crust from refrigerator; let stand at room temperature until just pliable. Unroll crust on a lightly floured surface; roll with a floured rolling pin. Using a 4-inch round cookie cutter (preferably ridged), cut out as many circles as possible. Transfer rounds to prepared sheet. Gather any dough scraps, reroll and cut more rounds.

2. For filling: In a small bowl, whisk brown sugar, cinnamon and flour. Spoon about 1 tablespoon filling onto one half of each circle of dough. Using a brush or your fingers, brush a little cold water around the circumference of the dough, and fold it in half, creating a semicircle. Seal the pie, and make a decorative edge by pressing the edges of the dough together with the tines of a fork. Repeat process with remaining dough. Refrigerate pies for 30 minutes.

3. Preheat oven to 350°F. Remove chilled pies from refrigerator, cut a small slit in each and lightly brush with egg yolk wash. Bake for 18 to 20 minutes, until light golden. Transfer to a wire rack to cool.

4. For frosting: In a medium bowl, whisk confectioners' sugar and cinnamon. Whisk in vanilla and cream until of drizzling consistency. Pour over cooled pies.

TIP: Alter the fillings according to the kids' favorite toaster-pasty flavors. Some ideas: mini-chocolate chips, Nutella, strawberry jam.

MAKES 8

1 refrigerated pie crust

1 large egg yolk mixed with 1 tablespoon cream, for wash

FILLING

⅓ cup brown sugar

1 teaspoon ground cinnamon

2 teaspoons all-purpose flour

FROSTING

½ cup confectioners' sugar

½ teaspoon ground cinnamon

½ teaspoon vanilla extract

1 tablespoon plus 2 teaspoons heavy cream or half-and-half

German Chocolate Oatmeal Cookies in a Jar

MAKES 50

JAR

1½ cups chopped pecans

2 cups all-purpose flour

1 teaspoon baking powder

1 teaspoon baking soda

1 teaspoon salt

1 cup light brown sugar

1 cup granulated sugar

2 cups sweetened coconut flakes

2 cups semisweet chocolate chips

TO ADD

1 cup (2 sticks) unsalted butter

2 large eggs

2 teaspoons vanilla extract

TIP: No need to limit yourself to canning jars. Any glass jar will do here to show off the ingredients.

Kids will enjoy layering the ingredients in the jars—but not as much as they will enjoy eating the chewy, hearty cookies.

1. Preheat oven to 325°F. Spread pecans on a rimmed baking sheet. Toast for 8 minutes, stirring often. Let cool.

2. In a medium bowl, combine flour, baking powder, soda and salt. Spoon into the bottom of a quart-size canning jar. Layer brown and granulated sugars on top of flour mixture. Press down a layer of plastic film that fits just inside the jar (this will keep the mix-ins separate from the dry ingredients). Add coconut, chocolate chips and toasted pecans.

3. Firmly screw lid on jar. Print out the following directions and attach to the jar:

German Chocolate Oatmeal Cookies

1. Preheat oven to 350°F. Line a baking sheet with parchment paper.

2. Pour coconut, chocolate chips and nuts into a small bowl, set aside. Spoon brown and white sugar into a mixing bowl, add 1 cup (2 sticks) unsalted butter and beat until light and fluffy. Beat in 2 large eggs and 2 teaspoons vanilla extract until combined. Pour oatmeal and flour mixture from jar into bowl; mix until blended. Stir in coconut, chocolate chips and nuts. Drop by spoonfuls onto prepared sheet, about 2 inches apart. Bake for 10 minutes, until lightly browned around the edges. Transfer to a wire rack to cool.

Homemade Chocolate Sandwich Cookies with Mint Filling

America's favorite cookie—fresh from your kitchen! You'll feel better knowing what's inside your cookies. More good news: When *you* make the filling, you can slather on as much as you want!

1. For cookies: In a large bowl with electric mixer on low speed, mix flour, cocoa, *both* sugars, baking soda, baking powder and salt until blended. Still on low speed, add butter pieces and egg; mix until dough comes together. Cover bowl and refrigerate for at least 1 hour or overnight.

2. Preheat oven to 350°F. Line 2 baking sheets with parchment paper. Scoop rounded teaspoons of batter; roll between your palms into small balls. Place on prepared sheets; slightly flatten the balls. Bake for 9 minutes, until firm and slightly cracked. Transfer to wire racks to cool.

3. For filling: In a large bowl with electric mixer on high speed, beat butter and shortening until combined. Gradually beat in confectioners' sugar and *both* extracts. Increase speed to high; beat for 3 minutes until light and fluffy.

4. Spread filling between 2 cooled cookies. Store cookies tightly covered.

TIP: Don't like mint? Omit the peppermint extract for a classic vanilla filling.

MAKES 25 TO 30 SANDWICH COOKIES

COOKIES

1 cup all-purpose flour

½ cup unsweetened cocoa

1 cup granulated sugar

¼ cup confectioners' sugar

1 teaspoon baking soda

¼ teaspoon baking powder

¼ teaspoon salt

10 tablespoons (1¼ sticks) unsalted butter, at room temperature

1 large egg

FILLING

4 tablespoons (½ stick) unsalted butter, at room temperature

¼ cup shortening

2 cups confectioners' sugar

1 teaspoon vanilla extract

½ teaspoon peppermint extract

Blueberry Crumb Bars

MAKES 24

BARS

3 cups all-purpose flour

1 cup granulated sugar

1 teaspoon baking powder

¼ teaspoon salt

2 teaspoons grated lemon zest (from 1 lemon)

1 cup (2 sticks) cold unsalted butter, cut into chunks, plus more for pan

1 large egg

FILLING

¼ cup granulated sugar

1 tablespoon cornstarch

3 cups frozen or fresh blueberries (about 12 ounces)

1 tablespoon fresh lemon juice

This recipe works well with frozen blueberries, so you can make it anytime of the year.

1. Preheat oven to 375°F. Line a 9-by-13-inch baking pan with foil or parchment paper, overhanging edges to serve as handles. Lightly butter foil.

2. For bars: In a food processor, pulse flour, sugar, baking powder, salt and lemon zest until combined. Add butter pieces and egg; pulse until dough resembles crumbly wet sand. Pat half of dough into the prepared pan.

3. For filling: In a medium bowl, stir together sugar and cornstarch. Gently fold in berries and lemon juice. Spread blueberry mixture evenly over crust, leaving a ½-inch border around the edges. Crumble remaining dough over berries.

4. Bake for 40 minutes, until top is golden brown and crust is firm. Transfer to a wire rack to cool completely. Use foil handles to lift bars from pan. Sprinkle with powdered sugar. Cover and store in refrigerator.

TIP: Store bars in the refrigerator; they become soft and lose their buttery crunch at room temperature.

Sweet-and-Salty Caramel Popcorn

MAKES 5 CUPS

4 cups plain popped popcorn (from about 2 microwave bags)

1½ cups peanuts or almonds

1 cup brown sugar

½ cup (1 stick) unsalted butter, plus more for pan

¼ cup light corn syrup

½ teaspoon vanilla extract

¼ teaspoon baking soda

Salt

Kids will love this homemade treat—just keep little hands away from the hot caramel.

1 Preheat oven to 250°F. Line 2 large rimmed baking sheets with foil; lightly butter foil or coat with nonstick spray. Spread popcorn and nuts on prepared sheets.

2 In a medium saucepan (preferably nonstick) over medium heat, combine brown sugar, butter and corn syrup. Bring to a boil, stirring occasionally. Let simmer for 5 minutes, stirring constantly. Remove from heat; stir in vanilla and baking soda. The mixture will bubble. Immediately drizzle hot caramel over the popcorn on the pans; folding mixture to coat.

3 Bake popcorn for 50 minutes, stirring often. Switch trays from top to bottom in oven halfway through cooking.

4 Lift foil from pans; place on wire racks. Let cool completely. Season with salt to taste.

5 Store in airtight containers.

TIP: Keep a close eye on the baking caramel to make sure it doesn't burn.

Hot Roasted Chestnuts

Roasting chestnuts is a holiday tradition meant to be passed down to future generations. Eat the rich nuts as a snack, an ice cream topping or stir them into your stuffing.

1½ pounds whole chestnuts

3 tablespoons water

1. Preheat oven to 400°F. With a very sharp knife, cut an X in the rounded side of each chestnut; cut through the shell but not into the meat of the nut. Place chestnuts in an ovenproof skillet, preferably nonstick. Cover and roast 15 minutes, shaking the pan often. Add water: roast 15 more minutes, until chestnuts are tender.

2. Wrap chestnuts in a clean heavy towel; let sit for about 5 minutes. When just cool enough to handle, crush chestnuts (still in the towel) with the bottom of a heavy pan to help release skins from nuts. Unwrap the towel; peel the skins from the meat.

> **TIP:** Chestnuts peel best while still warm. If they have cooled and you are unable to peel, blast them in the microwave for 20 seconds to soften the skins.

Roasted Root Vegetable Pizza

SERVES 4

½ small butternut squash (about 1½ pounds), peeled and cut into 1-inch cubes

½ pound boiling or red potatoes, cut into 1-inch cubes

½ pound carrots, peeled and cut into 1-inch chunks

½ pound beets, peeled and cut into 1-inch cubes

5 garlic cloves, crushed

3 tablespoons olive oil

1 tablespoon unsalted butter

Salt and black pepper

Cornmeal, for pan

1 pound prepared pizza dough

2 cups shredded mozzarella cheese

¾ cup ricotta cheese

This colorful meal is a great way to get kids to eat their vegetables. Get a head start by roasting the vegetables one day in advance.

1. Preheat oven to 400°F. Lightly coat 2 baking sheets with cooking spray.

2. In a large bowl, combine all chopped vegetables, garlic, 2 tablespoons of the oil, butter, salt and pepper; toss to coat. Spread in a single layer onto prepared sheets. Bake for 45 minutes, until tender and lightly browned, stirring and turning vegetable mixture occasionally. Remove sheets from oven; maintain oven temperature.

3. Lightly coat a large baking sheet with remaining 1 tablespoon oil; sprinkle with cornmeal. Roll out dough into a 12-by-16-inch oval; transfer to prepared sheet.

4. Sprinkle dough with half of the mozzarella. Evenly scatter vegetable mixture on top of the cheese. Scoop up ricotta with a spoon; drop dollops over vegetables. Cover with remaining mozzarella. Bake for 30 minutes, until crust is golden and cheese melted. Rotate baking sheet from front to back halfway through baking.

TIP: Save time and hassle by using frozen chopped winter squash.

Wintertime Pulled Pork Sandwiches

This makes a slightly sweet, not-too-spicy, kid-friendly sandwich filling. Add more hot sauce to turn up the heat.

1. Preheat oven to 350°F. Cut pork roast in half lengthwise; place 2 pieces side-by-side in a large Dutch oven or heavy pot with lid.

2. For rub: In a small bowl, combine all ingredients. Rub over pork, covering all sides. Let sit 10 minutes.

3. Add 1½ cups water to pot, or until water comes about halfway up the sides of the meat. Tightly cover pot with aluminum foil, then lid. Place in oven, roast 2½ hours, until pork is very tender and falling apart.

4. Transfer pork to a cutting board. Carefully peel away and discard any visible fat. Using two forks, pull meat apart until shredded.

5. For sauce: In a large bowl, combine all ingredients until blended. Add shredded pork; stir until coated with sauce. Season to taste with salt and pepper. Spoon meat onto rolls.

TIP: Look for cuts labeled Boston Butt, Picnic Roast or Pork Shoulder. Make sure it's a boneless roast.

SERVES 8

3-pound boneless pork shoulder, trimmed of excess fat

Salt and black pepper

8 rolls or buns

RUB

4 garlic cloves, chopped

2 tablespoons mustard

1 tablespoon sweet paprika

1 teaspoon liquid smoke

1 teaspoon dried oregano

Salt and black pepper

SAUCE

¾ cup ketchup

2 tablespoons molasses

1 tablespoon Worcestershire sauce

2 teaspoons hot sauce

Chili for a Crowd

SERVES 10

2 tablespoons olive oil

1 medium onion, chopped

1 can (6 ounces) tomato paste

8 garlic cloves, chopped

3 pounds ground chuck

6 tablespoons chili powder

2 tablespoons unsweetened cocoa

1 tablespoon ground cumin

½ teaspoon dried thyme

1 can (28 ounces) crushed tomatoes with added puree

1 can (14¾ ounces) reduced-sodium chicken broth

1 bottle (12 ounces) beer, or equal amount beef broth

1 can (16 ounces) red kidney beans, drained

Garnishes: Sour cream, chopped scallions or onions, chopped fresh cilantro

Easy to make and full of flavor—this is sure to become your go-to chili recipe. A bottle of beer adds a depth of flavor, but feel free to substitute beef broth if you like.

1. Warm oil in a large Dutch oven or heavy saucepan over medium-high heat. Add onion; cook for 8 minutes, until softened, stirring. Add tomato paste and garlic; cook for 1 minute, until paste darkens, stirring. Add beef; cook for 5 minutes, until no longer pink, stirring.

2. Stir in chili powder, cocoa, cumin and thyme. Mix in tomatoes, chicken broth and beer. Bring to a simmer; reduce heat and cook for 1 hour and 15 minutes, until thickened to desired consistency. Stir often and add water, if needed, during cooking.

3. Stir in beans; cook for 5 minutes, until warmed through. Season to taste with salt and pepper. Serve with desired garnishes.

TIP: Like all good chilis, this one can be prepared up to 3 days ahead. In fact, the flavor improves overnight.

Sloppy Joe Pizza

Remember how much you loved Sloppy Joes and pizza as a child? Here, a perfect combination of two quintessential kid foods. Make it for your kids, grandkids or yourself tonight!

SERVES 4 TO 6

1. Preheat oven to 400°F. Lightly coat a large baking sheet with cooking spray; sprinkle with cornmeal.

2. Warm oil in a large skillet over medium heat. Add bell pepper and onion; cook for 6 minutes, stirring. Add garlic; cook for 30 seconds. Stir in beef; cook for 7 minutes, until meat is browned.

3. Stir in ketchup, brown sugar, vinegar, dry mustard and Worcestershire sauce. Reduce heat; simmer for 5 minutes, stirring often. Add a splash of water if mixture seems too thick. Season with salt and pepper.

4. Roll out dough to a 12-by-16-inch oval; transfer to prepared baking sheet. Evenly cover dough with meat mixture; sprinkle with cheese. Bake for 25 minutes, or until crust is golden and cheese melted.

TIP: Most supermarkets carry prepared pizza dough in the dairy section. Another option: Stop by your favorite pizza parlor and ask to buy a ball of unbaked dough.

Cooking spray and cornmeal, for pan

2 tablespoons olive oil

1 red or green bell pepper, finely diced

½ small onion, chopped

1 garlic clove, crushed

1 pound ground beef

1 cup ketchup

2 tablespoons brown sugar

2 teaspoons apple-cider vinegar

2 teaspoons dry mustard powder

2 teaspoons Worcestershire sauce

Salt and black pepper

1 pound prepared pizza dough

1 cup shredded Monterey Jack cheese

Ice Krispie Snowmen

MAKES 6

No snow? No problem. Bring winter fun indoors with these sweet snowmen that kids can make and decorate themselves.

4 tablespoons (½ stick) unsalted butter, plus more for pan

1 bag (10 ounces) mini marshmallows

5 cups crispy rice cereal

1½ cups sweetened shredded coconut

Prepared vanilla icing, as needed

Decorations: mini chocolate chips, candy corn, black gumdrops, peppermint patties, colorful fruit leather

1. Line a baking sheet with parchment or waxed paper. Place butter and marshmallows in a glass bowl; microwave in 30-second intervals, until fully melted, stirring often. Place cereal in a large bowl; fold in marshmallow mixture until coated.

2. Place coconut in a medium deep bowl. Butter your hands lightly. Scoop up a spoonful of the mixture and drop into coconut. Using your hands, roll each mound in coconut, pressing into a tight ball as you roll. Make 18 balls: 6 large, 6 medium and 6 small. Using a dab of icing to stick balls together, form 6 snowmen. Set the snowmen upright on prepared baking sheet.

3. Decorate snowmen as desired. Some ideas: chocolate chips for eyes, tip of candy corn for nose, gumdrop placed atop mint patty for hat. Cut a strip of fruit leather for scarf. Use icing to "glue" candy onto snowmen.

Soothing Scented Lip Balm

MAKES 4 TINS (½ OUNCE EACH)

Who wouldn't love a homemade lip balm? Scent combinations to try: peppermint-eucalyptus, rose-vanilla. Find all the ingredients at online craft supply stores.

4 tablespoons sweet almond oil

2 tablespoons beeswax pearls (also called pellets or pastilles)

2 tablespoons pure shea butter

10 to 15 drops essential oils

4 drops vitamin E

4 ½-ounce lip balm tins

Combine almond oil, beeswax and shea butter in a glass measuring cup set in a pot of simmering water. Warm until melted, whisking often. Remove from heat; whisk in essential oils and vitamin E. Quickly pour mixture into lip balm tins. Let balms cool completely until solid, about 20 minutes. Write the name of the scent on a sticker that fits on the lid. Store in a cool, dry place.

Easy Family Dinners

The holiday season is one of the busiest times of the year for me and I'm sure it is for you as well. At my house, it starts with the decorations. Then there are the Christmas Teas and Open Houses, all of which require sending out invitations, baking, cooking, cleaning. Plus menu planning, card sending, list making—and let's not forget the shopping, the search for that all-important special gift (or gifts!).

Years ago, I went on a mad search for a Cabbage Patch doll for my daughter. There was none to be found anywhere but that doesn't mean I didn't look. I raced from store to store, hoping, praying for that doll. I never did find one, not at Christmas. Jody had to wait until her birthday in February. More recently, one of the grandchildren wanted a Tickle Me Elmo. Unfortunately it was the same scenario.

Another Christmas task—my Christmas letter. From the very first year Wayne and I were married, I've written one. In fact, it was the reactions from family and friends to my yearly updates that led me to believe I should try my hand at books. That letter-writing tradition continues. (The heroine in *There's Something About Christmas* turns it into a profession, too—writing Christmas letters for other people!)

Wayne and I have never lived near either of our families, so there are always packages to box up and ship, too.

Are you tired yet?

The last thing I want to do during the holiday season is worry about what I'm going to put on the table for dinner. I can always pick up something convenient on my way home from the office and I'll admit I've done that, but too much fast food leaves a great deal to be desired—in terms of nutrition *and* taste. One of my favorite shortcuts, however, involves the rotisserie chicken I can buy at the grocery store. It can be used in dozens of recipes.

Here's another shortcut. . . . My absolute favorite kitchen appliance is my Crock-Pot. I drag it out two or three times a week. During the winter, Wayne and I especially enjoy hearty soups. One result of having raised a large family is that I can't seem to cook for two; everything I prepare, even now, feeds six or more. I can't stop myself! My daughter Jody, who lives only a block away, often stops by for some leftovers on her way home. There's always enough to feed her family, too. Sharing with them is gratifying—and certainly counts as a shortcut for her, which is a good thing, since Jazmine and James are often busy with sports. Jody and the kids are grateful to be so close to Grandma's and *I'm* grateful to have someone I can give the extras to.

If ever there's a time of year when quick and easy recipes are needed, it's the holidays. I know you're going to enjoy these, and you'll find that they will become part of your repertoire *every* day of the year and not just at Christmas.

Crock-Pot Chicken Chili

SERVES 8

1 pound dried Great Northern or cannellini beans, soaked overnight

3 cups reduced-sodium chicken broth, warmed

1 large onion, chopped

3 garlic cloves, minced

1 jalapeño pepper, minced

1 tablespoon plus 1 teaspoon chili powder

2 teaspoons ground cumin

Salt and black pepper

1 pound (about 3 cups, chopped) cooked chicken or turkey meat

1 box (10 ounces) frozen corn kernels

2 cups shredded Monterey Jack cheese

1 tablespoon fresh lime juice

Garnishes: Sour cream, chopped fresh cilantro, salsa, chopped scallions

Serve this creamy, slightly spicy stew with fresh warmed flour tortillas or tortilla chips.

1. Combine beans and warm broth in a large slow cooker; let sit for 10 minutes. Stir in onion, garlic, jalapeño, chili powder, cumin, salt and pepper. Cover and cook on low heat for 10 hours, or until beans are tender.

2. Stir in chicken, corn and cheese. Cook for 10 minutes, until chicken and corn are warmed through and cheese is melted. Add lime juice and season to taste with salt and pepper. Garnish as desired.

TIP: Crock-Pot cooking time can vary widely depending on your machine. Be sure to cook this until the beans are tender but not mushy.

Shown on page 189.

Homestyle Slow-Cook Pot Roast

The best cut for pot roast is a chuck-eye roast. Some butchers actually label this cut "Pot Roast." It should have a twine wrapped around the center.

1. Season roast with salt and pepper; sprinkle with flour. Warm 1 tablespoon of the oil in a Dutch oven or large heavy skillet over medium-high heat. Add meat and brown on all sides, about 8 to 10 minutes. Transfer meat to a platter. Add ½ cup wine to skillet; cook for 2 minutes, until wine cooks off, stirring with a wooden spoon. Scrape any juices in skillet over meat on platter.

2. Warm remaining tablespoon oil in skillet over medium heat. Add onions and carrots; cook for 5 minutes, stirring often. Spoon vegetables into slow cooker; top with roast and any juices that have collected on the platter. Add the remaining cup of wine, broth, tomato sauce, garlic, thyme and bay leaf to the slow cooker. The liquid should come about halfway up the sides of the meat. Cover the pot and cook on low for 10 to 12 hours, until the meat and vegetables are tender. The meat should fall apart when nudged with a fork.

3. Transfer roast to a cutting board. Pour vegetables and sauce into a bowl. Let sit for 5 minutes; remove bay leaf and skim off any fat from gravy. Slice meat; serve with gravy and vegetables. Season to taste with salt and pepper.

SERVES 6 TO 8

3- to 4-pound chuck roast, tied with twine

Salt and black pepper

3 tablespoons all-purpose flour

2 tablespoons olive oil

1½ cups red wine, divided

2 medium onions, chopped

4 carrots, peeled and sliced

1 cup reduced-sodium beef broth

1 cup tomato sauce

1 garlic clove, minced

1 tablespoon chopped fresh thyme

1 bay leaf

TIP: Browning the roast before cooking seals in the juices and gives a flavorful brown crust.

Pasta Puttanesca with Eggplant

SERVES 6

12 ounces spaghetti or fettuccine

3 tablespoons olive oil

1 medium eggplant, diced

4 garlic cloves, minced

¼ to ½ teaspoon red pepper flakes

2 anchovy fillets, minced

1 can (28 ounces) crushed tomatoes with basil

½ cup black olives (such as Kalamata), pitted and chopped

1 tablespoon red-wine vinegar

2 teaspoons drained capers

¾ cup chopped fresh parsley or basil

Salt

This super-simple sauce cooks in the same amount of time it takes to boil the pasta. More good news: Most of the ingredients come straight from the pantry.

1. Cook pasta according to package directions. Drain.

2. Warm 2 tablespoons of the oil in a large heavy skillet over medium-low heat. Add eggplant; cook for 8 minutes, until softened, stirring often. Transfer to a large serving bowl.

3. Warm remaining oil in same skillet (no need to wash) over medium-low heat. Add garlic, red pepper flakes and anchovies; cook for 30 seconds, stirring often. Stir in tomatoes and browned eggplant; bring to a simmer and cook for 6 minutes, until thickened. Add olives, vinegar, capers and parsley.

4. Place drained pasta in serving bowl. Add sauce; toss to coat. Season with salt to taste.

TIP: When anchovies are incorporated into a cooked sauce, they add a salty, briny, but not fishy, flavor. Because of the fish's saltiness, be sure to taste test the sauce before adding salt.

Not-so-Spicy Sesame Peanut Noodles

Serve this family-friendly pasta dish warm from the pot, or cold, in the style of Chinese restaurants.

SERVES 4 TO 6

1. In a blender or food processor, puree peanut butter, soy sauce, water, ginger, garlic, vinegar, sesame oil, honey and pepper flakes until smooth and the consistency of heavy cream. Transfer sauce to a large serving bowl.

2. Cook pasta according to package directions. Reserve ½ cup of the pasta cooking water. Drain pasta and rinse well.

3. Add pasta to dressing in bowl. Toss well, adding reserved pasta water as needed. Garnish pasta with scallions, cucumber and sesame seeds; serve immediately.

TIP: Asian, or dark sesame oil is dark in color and intensely flavored. Find it in the Asian food section of your market. It is sometimes called "toasted" sesame oil.

½ cup smooth peanut butter

¼ cup reduced-sodium soy sauce

2 tablespoons warm water

1 tablespoon chopped and peeled fresh ginger

1 garlic clove, chopped

2 tablespoons rice-wine vinegar

2 tablespoons Asian (dark) sesame oil

1 tablespoon honey or brown sugar

¼ to ½ teaspoon red pepper flakes or chili garlic paste

1 pound linguine or thin spaghetti

2 scallions, thinly sliced

1 cucumber, peeled and cut into ⅛-inch-thick strips

3 tablespoons toasted sesame seeds

Chicken Marsala with Mushrooms and Shallots

SERVES 4

4 boneless, skinless chicken breast halves, trimmed

⅓ cup all-purpose flour

Salt and black pepper

1 tablespoon olive oil

2 tablespoons unsalted butter

2 slices bacon, chopped

12 ounces white mushrooms, sliced

1 shallot, chopped

1 garlic clove, minced

2 teaspoons chopped fresh thyme

1 cup sweet Marsala wine

1 tablespoon fresh lemon juice

Golden chicken is covered with a creamy, savory mushroom sauce in this classic Italian dish.

1 Place a chicken breast on a square of plastic wrap or waxed paper, cover with another sheet and pound until thin but not broken. Repeat with remaining breasts. Place flour in a shallow bowl. Sprinkle chicken with salt and pepper and dredge in flour, shaking off any excess.

2 Warm oil and 1 tablespoon of the butter in a large heavy skillet over medium-high heat. Once the butter has melted, add chicken to pan and cook for 5 minutes, until golden brown. Turn; cook for 4 minutes. (Chicken will not be cooked through.)

3 Add chopped bacon to same skillet over medium heat. Cook for 2 minutes, stirring. Add mushrooms; cook for 5 minutes, until tender and golden brown, stirring often. (Add oil if the pan seems too dry.)

4 Add shallot, garlic and thyme; cook for 2 minutes, until shallot softens, stirring. Add Marsala; increase heat and bring to a simmer. Cook for about 3 minutes, until sauce is reduced and thickened. Return chicken to skillet, along with any juices that have collected on the plate. Add lemon juice and remaining tablespoon butter. Warm through, stirring to combine and turning the chicken to finish cooking and to coat with sauce.

TIP: Cooking time may vary due to the wide range of chicken breast sizes available. Test for doneness by making a small cut in the thickest part of the breast with a sharp knife to ensure meat is not pink.

Fried Chicken BLT Salad

SERVES 4

4 slices bacon

2/3 cup all-purpose flour

2 large eggs, beaten with
1 tablespoon water

1 cup Panko bread crumbs

1/2 cup grated Parmesan cheese

4 chicken breast halves, lightly
pounded to 1/2-inch thick

Salt and black pepper

Peanut or vegetable oil, for frying

SALAD

Romaine lettuce

Cherry tomatoes, halved

1/2 cup shaved Parmesan cheese

Prepared salad dressing or extra-
virgin olive oil

Please the whole family with this main-dish salad. Remember that you don't want to crowd the chicken in the pan. All the breasts will fit into a 12-inch skillet; any smaller and you'll need to use two skillets.

1 In a large heavy skillet over medium heat, cook bacon until crisp. Transfer to a paper-towel-lined plate to drain and cool. Retain drippings in skillet.

2 Set up 3 shallow bowls for dredging chicken. Fill 1 bowl with flour, 1 with beaten eggs and water, and 1 with a mixture of Panko and grated cheese. Season chicken with salt and pepper; dredge lightly in flour, then egg wash, then bread crumbs, coating both sides. Lay breaded chicken on a platter and refrigerate for at least 1 hour.

3 Add oil to bacon drippings in skillet to reach about a 1/4-inch up the side of the pan. Set over medium-high heat until hot. Pan is hot enough when a piece of bread dropped in oil sizzles. Add chicken; cook for 5 minutes on each side, until golden brown, crispy and just cooked through. Transfer breasts to a paper-towel-lined cutting board to drain. Sprinkle with salt. Discard paper towels. Slice breasts on the diagonal.

4 Coarsely chop bacon. In a large serving bowl, toss lettuce, tomatoes, shaved cheese and bacon with dressing or olive oil. Divide salad among serving plates; top with chicken slices.

TIP: Panko is a super-flaky bread crumb originally used in Japanese cuisine. It is now widely available in specialty stores and large supermarkets. If you can't find it, substitute traditional bread crumbs.

Quick and Easy Taco Salad

The good thing about making your own taco salad is that you can add only the fixings you like.

1. Warm oil in a large heavy skillet over medium heat. Add onion, chili powder and cumin; cook for 6 minutes, until softened, stirring occasionally. Add beef and garlic; cook for 5 minutes, until meat is no longer pink, stirring occasionally. Spoon off any excess oil. Add tomato sauce, salt and pepper; cook for 3 minutes until meat is cooked through, stirring.

2. Meanwhile, divide chopped lettuce among 4 serving bowls. Place avocado, lettuce, tomato, shredded cheese, beans and sour cream in separate bowls. Ladle beef into serving bowls; allow diners to create their own salads. Serve with tortilla chips.

TIP: To easily remove an avocado pit, firmly stab the seed with the blade of a sharp knife, then twist the knife and lift it out of the avocado, with the blade still stuck in the seed.

SERVES 4

FILLING

1 tablespoon olive oil

1 small onion, chopped

2 teaspoons chili powder

2 teaspoons ground cumin

1¼ pounds ground chuck

2 garlic cloves, minced

1 can (8 ounces) tomato sauce

Salt and black pepper

SALAD

1 small head iceberg lettuce, thinly sliced (about 8 cups)

1 firm-ripe avocado, cut into chunks

1 large tomato, diced or 1½ cups salsa

1 cup shredded extra-sharp cheddar cheese

1 cup canned black beans, drained and rinsed

1 cup sour cream

Tortilla chips

Garlic Shrimp Stir-fry with Swiss Chard

SERVES 4

1 pound frozen, peeled and deveined shrimp, thawed

2 tablespoons peanut or olive oil

4 teaspoons minced and peeled fresh ginger

3 garlic cloves, minced

Salt

Dash crushed red pepper

2 tablespoons reduced-sodium soy sauce

2 tablespoons fresh lime juice

1 tablespoon brown sugar

1 bunch Swiss chard (about 1½ pounds), cleaned, trimmed and coarsely chopped

2 scallions, thinly sliced

Serve this colorful hearty dish over rice. If chard isn't available, use kale or spinach.

1. In a large bowl, combine shrimp, 1 tablespoon of the oil, half the ginger, half the garlic, salt and a dash of crushed red pepper. Marinate for at least 15 minutes or up to 1 hour.

2. In a small bowl, whisk soy sauce, lime juice and sugar.

3. Warm a large nonstick skillet over high heat. Add shrimp; cook for 2 minutes, until shrimp are just opaque in center, stirring constantly. Transfer to a serving platter.

4. Warm remaining oil in same skillet over medium heat; add Swiss chard; stir-fry for 5 minutes, until tender. Add remaining garlic and ginger; stir-fry for 30 seconds. Return shrimp to skillet; pour in soy mixture. Stir-fry until coated and warmed through. Garnish servings with sliced scallions.

TIP: Use a big skillet here; the chard leaves need a lot of room. They do cook down considerably.

Pan-Roasted Flank Steak with Ginger-Sesame Marinade

SERVES 4

1 flank steak (about 1⅓ pounds)

Salt and black pepper

2 teaspoons olive oil

MARINADE

2 tablespoons Asian (dark) sesame oil

1 tablespoon olive oil

2 garlic cloves, minced

2 scallions, thinly sliced

1 tablespoon minced, peeled fresh ginger

Letting the steak rest after pan-roasting is crucial—it allows the meat to continue cooking to the proper temperature and allows the juices to redistribute throughout the steak.

1 For marinade: Combine all ingredients in a blender or food processor; puree until blended into a paste, scraping down sides of the bowl as needed.

2 Using a fork, poke holes on both sides of steak. Place steak in a glass or nonreactive bowl or baking dish; season with salt. Add marinade; flip to coat meat. Cover bowl with plastic wrap and refrigerate at least 1 hour or overnight.

3 Preheat oven to 425°F; adjust oven rack to middle position. Using paper towels, wipe marinade off steak; season with pepper. Warm oil in a large heavy ovenproof skillet over medium-high heat until smoking. Cook steak for 4 minutes per side, until browned. Transfer skillet to oven; roast for about 5 minutes, until slightly less done than desired. Transfer steak to cutting board, tent loosely with foil, and let rest for 5 minutes. Using a sharp knife, thinly slice steak against the grain.

TIP: For a beautifully browned crust, blot the wet marinade from the steak before cooking. If there is too much liquid on the meat, it will steam rather than brown.

Roast Pork Tenderloin with Dijon-Molasses Glaze

Serve this savory pork with roasted potatoes or a seasoned rice dish.

1. Preheat oven to 350°F. Warm oil in a large heavy ovenproof skillet over medium-high heat. Season pork with salt and pepper; sprinkle with oregano. Sear pork for 8 minutes, turning until browned on all sides.

2. Meanwhile, in a small skillet set over medium heat, whisk molasses and mustard until blended. Add orange juice and vinegar; bring to a simmer. Cook for 5 minutes, until thickened to a glaze.

3. Brush seared pork with glaze. Transfer skillet to oven; cook for 18 minutes, until a thermometer inserted at the thickest part registers 150°F. Transfer to a platter; thinly slice.

TIP: Pork tenderloin often comes two to a package. Look for large cuts for this recipe; you want a piece that's more than a pound.

SERVES 4

1 tablespoon olive oil

1 large pork tenderloin (about 1¼ pounds)

Salt and black pepper

2 tablespoons chopped fresh oregano

¼ cup molasses

2 tablespoons Dijon mustard

3 tablespoons orange juice

1 tablespoon apple-cider vinegar

Seared Salmon with White Bean Ragout

Keep your eyes open for sales at your fish market—salmon can often be found for less than the price of a steak.

SERVES 4

1. Warm oil in a large heavy skillet over medium heat. Season fish with salt and pepper; sprinkle with Wondra. Cook fillet for 3 minutes per side (fish will not be cooked through). Using a spatula, transfer fish to a platter.

2. Add tomatoes, beans, garlic, rosemary and ½ cup water to the same skillet over medium-high heat. Cook for 3 minutes. Reduce heat to low; stir in vinegar. Nestle fillets in the bean mixture; cover skillet and cook for 3 minutes or until the fish is just cooked through. Fish is done when the flesh flakes when tested with a fork. Serve fish in shallow bowls; ladle beans and sauce over fillets.

TIP: Wondra is a brand name for instant, finely ground flour. This super-light flour is often used in gravy-making because it thickens without lumping. It's also great for sprinkling over fish fillets before pan-searing, since it creates a nice golden crust.

2 tablespoons olive oil

1¼ pounds salmon fillet (about ¾-inch thick), cut into 4 equal pieces

Salt and black pepper

2 tablespoons Wondra or all-purpose flour

1 pint cherry or pear tomatoes

1 can (16 ounces) cannellini or other white beans, drained and rinsed

2 garlic cloves, minced

1 tablespoon minced fresh rosemary

1 tablespoon red-wine vinegar

Penne with Glazed Winter Squash and Garlic Sausage

SERVES 4

1 small butternut squash (about 1½ pounds), peeled, seeded and cut in ½-inch dice

1 pound Italian sausage (preferably with garlic and herbs), casing removed and thickly sliced or crumbled into large chunks

4 garlic cloves, chopped

Salt and black pepper

1 tablespoon chopped fresh thyme

1 tablespoon olive oil

12 ounces penne or rigatoni

¾ cup grated Romano or Parmesan cheese

¼ cup chopped fresh parsley

This is a perfect homestyle meal for a cold winter night. Add any flavor of sausage you like, or leave it out for a vegetarian meal.

1 Preheat oven to 400°F. Line a baking sheet with foil. In a bowl, toss squash cubes and sausage chunks with garlic, salt, pepper, thyme and oil until squash is coated with oil. Spread mixture evenly on prepared baking sheet; roast for 30 minutes, or until squash is tender and sausage is cooked through and lightly browned. Stir mixture occasionally. Transfer mixture to a large serving bowl. Keep warm.

2 Meanwhile, cook pasta according to package directions. Ladle about ½ cup cooking water from the cooking pot into the serving bowl. Drain pasta.

3 Toss hot pasta with the warm squash mixture, cheese and parsley. Season to taste with salt and pepper.

TIP: Save on prep time by using frozen squash chunks. Just make sure they have nothing added to them.

Chipotle Chicken Quesadillas

SERVES 4

1 roasted chicken, white meat only

1 tablespoon olive oil

1 small onion, finely chopped

1 teaspoon ground cumin

1 teaspoon ground coriander

1 canned chipotle pepper in adobo sauce, seeded and chopped (about 2 teaspoons)

1¼ cups canned diced tomatoes

1 teaspoon granulated sugar

Salt and black pepper

8 small flour tortillas

1 cup shredded Monterey Jack cheese

½ cup sour cream

1 scallion, thinly sliced

Serve these spicy wedges with a crisp green salad. Save time by using the meat from a cooked rotisserie chicken. You'll have leftover meat from the bird—save it for another meal.

1. Remove skin from chicken breasts; shred meat into a medium bowl. Reserve remaining meat for another use.

2. Warm oil in a medium nonstick saucepan over medium-low heat. Add onion; cook for 5 minutes, stirring. Add cumin, coriander, hot pepper, tomatoes and sugar. Cook for 5 minutes, stirring often. Transfer to bowl with chicken. Toss to coat; season to taste with salt and pepper.

3. Preheat oven to 400°F. Lightly coat 2 medium skillets with nonstick cooking spray; place over medium heat. Place a tortilla on each hot skillet. Top each with a quarter (about ½ cup) of the chicken mixture, a quarter (about ¼ cup) of the cheese and another tortilla. Cook until golden, pressing down on the tortilla. Carefully turn stacks; cook for 2 minutes, until bottom is golden and filling is hot. Transfer to a baking sheet; place in warm oven. Repeat with remaining tortillas, cheese and filling.

4. Cut hot quesadillas into wedges, top with sour cream and sprinkle with sliced scallion.

TIP: Chipotle chilies add a smoky punch of flavor without a lot of heat. Note that the recipe calls for 1 seeded pepper, not 1 can of peppers.

Steak Salad with Roasted Tomatoes, Frico and Baby Arugula

Skirt is an excellent choice for a quick weeknight dinner. Because it's a thin cut, it cooks quickly, yet retains its juicy and tender texture. Here, seared steak is paired with mellow roast tomatoes and frico, or Italian-style melted cheese disks.

1. For tomatoes: Preheat oven to 375°F. In a medium bowl, toss tomatoes with vinegar, salt and pepper. Roast for 18 to 20 minutes or until tomatoes burst and are spotted golden brown, shaking pan occasionally. Remove from oven; increase temperature to 400°F.

2. For frico: Line a baking sheet with parchment paper. Drop heaping tablespoons of grated Parmesan on prepared sheet, spacing cheese at least ½ inch apart. Using your fingers, spread out grated cheese to an even layer. (You should have about 8 rounds; reserve 2 tablespoons Parmesan for serving.) Bake for about 5 minutes until crisp and golden brown.

3. Meanwhile, warm the oil in a large heavy skillet over high heat until hot. Cook steak for 3 minutes per side, until charred and almost cooked through. Remove to cutting board (steak will finish cooking while it rests). Thinly slice on the diagonal.

4. For vinaigrette: In a large serving bowl, whisk vinegar and mustard until blended. Pour in oil, whisking until dressing thickens. Season with salt and pepper. Add greens and roasted tomatoes; gently toss to coat. Distribute salad evenly onto 4 serving plates. Top with steak slices and frico. Sprinkle salads with reserved grated Parmesan.

SERVES 4

1 tablespoon extra-virgin olive oil

1¼ pounds skirt steak

ROASTED TOMATOES AND FRICO

24 cherry or pear tomatoes

2 tablespoons sherry-wine or red-wine vinegar

Salt and black pepper

1 cup grated Parmesan cheese

VINAIGRETTE AND SALAD

3 tablespoons sherry-wine or red-wine vinegar

1 teaspoon Dijon mustard

¼ cup extra-virgin olive oil

Salt and black pepper

1 bag (4 ounces) baby arugula or mixed salad greens

TIP: Although the recipe calls for baby arugula, there are so many choices of packaged micro salad greens on the market; select one your family likes.

Creative Cards

A handmade card makes for an extra-special holiday greeting.

Winter Wonderland Tree Cards

Makes 1

You'll need a padded envelope and extra postage if you want to mail these touchable cards.

SUPPLIES

Textured or glitter cardstock

White cotton balls or squares

Clear glue

Thin stick

Silver dragées

1. Using cardstock, cut cards to desired size.

2. Using your fingers, stretch and shape cotton ball into the shape of a Christmas tree. The tree should fit on the top flap of the card. Glue the tree onto the card. Glue a short stick onto the bottom of the tree to look like a trunk. Glue silver dragées onto the tree for decoration. Let dry before using.

Retro Ornament Greetings

Makes 1

Search out vintage wrapping paper at tag sales throughout the year to make these simple yet sensational cards.

SUPPLIES

Drinking glass

Thick cardstock

Vintage or favorite wrapping paper

X-ACTO knife or scissors

Glue

Thin ribbon

1. Using a drinking glass, trace a circle onto cardstock. Add a small box at the top of the circle—this is the ornament top. Carefully cut out template. Place template on wrapping paper and trace out design. Cut out ornament shape from wrapping paper. Glue paper to template.

2. Using cardstock, cut cards to desired size. Punch holes in box atop ornament and at top of front flap of card. Tie ornament to card with ribbon.

Acknowledgments

After the success of the *Cedar Cove Cookbook* I was approached by my publisher about the possibility of doing a second. I knew immediately that it should revolve around Christmas. As you've probably realized, I'm big on the holidays, family and, you guessed it . . . food. I especially love a dish I can create in my own kitchen. If it involves the grandkids, all the better!

Deborah Brody, the executive editor for Harlequin Nonfiction, who was so instrumental in putting together the *Cedar Cove Cookbook,* was enthusiastic. I'd been impressed with Deb after our first cookbook venture, and she once again proved to be both skilled and insightful. She quickly recruited the talented Susie Ott, the recipe developer who'd scrutinized my recipes for the previous book, and did so for this one, and then put them to the test in her kitchen. Some of these recipes were written on scraps of paper passed to me by my mother; others I'd collected through the years. One, the special rice dish Mom served at Thanksgiving and Christmas every year, had never been written down. Susie had to develop the entire recipe based on my memories.

Susi Oberhelman, who did such a beautiful job of designing this book, and Catrine Kelty, the food stylist who worked with photographer Andy Ryan, also deserve thanks and applause.

In fact, not only will the recipes inspire you, the photography will, too. Andy did an amazing job—the dishes look as delicious as they taste. He was the photographer on my first cookbook, so I expected nothing less.

As always, a great deal of credit goes to my fabulous fiction editor, Paula Eykelhof. Paula has supported and encouraged my ideas for twenty-five years and this book is no exception.

Special thanks to my agent, Theresa Park, who embraced this idea from the first. Also to my wonderful family. Thank you, Wayne, for loving me enough to let me pursue my dream of one day publishing a book. To my children Jody, Jenny Adele, Ted and Dale, with thanks for gracing us with nine of the cutest grandkids in the universe and for all the memories we've created together in the kitchen.

This cookbook is about far more than the recipes, although they're very special and I promise you're going to enjoy them. I'm opening my home to you, sharing our holiday traditions, our kitchen and—most important—our hearts. My hope is that you'll savor this book, take these ideas and make them your own. Nothing brings family together more than gathering around a table when the meal has been prepared by loving hands.

Conversion Chart

WEIGHT

1 ounce	28 g
4 ounces or ¼ pound	113 g
⅓ pound	150 g
8 ounces or ½ pound	230 g
⅔ pound	300 g
12 ounces or ¾ pound	340 g
1 pound or 16 ounces	450 g
2 pounds	900 g
2.2 pounds	1 kilogram

TEMPERATURE

Fahrenheit	Celsius
212°	100°
250°	120°
275°	140°
300°	150°
325°	160°
350°	180°
375°	190°
400°	200°
425°	220°
450°	230°
475°	240°
500°	260°

VOLUME

1 teaspoon	5 mL	¾ cup or 6 fluid ounces	180 mL
1 tablespoon or ½ fluid ounce	15 mL	1 cup or 8 fluid ounces or ½ pint	240 mL
1 fluid ounce or ⅛ cup	30 mL	1½ cups or 12 fluid ounces	350 mL
¼ cup or 2 fluid ounces	60 mL	2 cups or 16 fluid ounces or 1 pint	475 mL
⅓ cup	80 mL	3 cups or 1½ pints	700 mL
½ cup or 4 fluid ounces	120 mL	4 cups or 2 pints or 1 quart	950 mL
⅔ cup	160 mL	4 quarts or 1 gallon	3.8 L

Index

My Recipes

TITLE

INGREDIENTS

PREPARATION

TITLE

INGREDIENTS

PREPARATION

TITLE

INGREDIENTS

PREPARATION

TITLE

INGREDIENTS

PREPARATION

TITLE

INGREDIENTS

PREPARATION

TITLE

INGREDIENTS

PREPARATION

TITLE

INGREDIENTS

PREPARATION

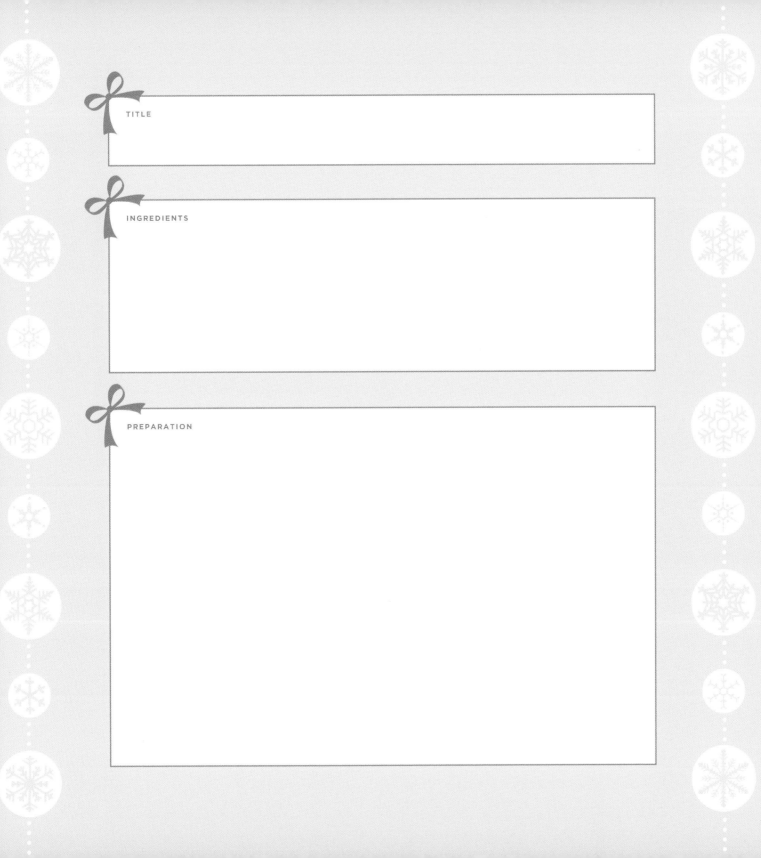

TITLE

INGREDIENTS

PREPARATION

TITLE

INGREDIENTS

PREPARATION

TITLE

INGREDIENTS

PREPARATION

TITLE

INGREDIENTS

PREPARATION

TITLE

INGREDIENTS

PREPARATION

TITLE

INGREDIENTS

PREPARATION

TITLE

INGREDIENTS

PREPARATION

TITLE

INGREDIENTS

PREPARATION

TITLE

INGREDIENTS

PREPARATION